ENCOUNTERS *with* GOD THROUGH DREAMS AND VISIONS

A JOURNEY...

"I bless the Lord who is my counsellor; even at night guides me"
Psalm 16:7

LANNI FIDES

Encounters with God Through Dreams and Visions

All Scripture verses and some reflections are from The New Community Bible, Catholic Edition, St Pauls Publications @2008 and are used by permission - Society of St Paul, Strathfield, NSW Australia.

The accounts in this book are based on actual events. Some names have been changed to protect privacy.

tellwell

Tellwell Talent
www.tellwell.ca

ISBN
978-0-2288-7320-4 (Hardcover)
978-0-2288-7321-1 (Paperback)
978-0-2288-7319-8 (eBook)

Table of Contents

Dedication

to

my loving husband, Stephen
our beloved children and families:

Jasmine & husband Jeremiah, children Jean & Jermaine
Matthew & wife Raelyn, children Raphael & Mae
Lily & husband Marty, children Christopher & Maya

my loving sister Jade
all relatives and friends

and

You, my readers

Acknowledgements

Deepest gratitude for the motivation, inspiration and support of:

my loving family

Catholic Church Parish of St. John 23rd Stanhope Gardens
and its Ministries of the Word and Special Religious Education,
NSW, Australia

Community of Couples for Christ Australia
and its Ministries
my Chapter-Seniors' Household,
NSW, Australia

Society of St Paul, NSW Australia

INTRODUCTION

Amazingly, I saw in the sky two intertwined hearts, not only coloured brightly in red but also the rest of the rainbow colours! This is one of my dreams revealed in this book!

Did I get a message from God through this dream? How did it affect my life and family? Take a break from the busyness of the world and simply feel the peace and joy in the presence of God!

This book will take you on a journey to the encounters with God, through the dreams and visions of selected biblical characters, prophets, and saints. This will be followed by my testimonial encounters with God! Does this sound like too much for you? Just give it a go and see!

How and when did I discover my prophetic gifts? How did God speak to me through dreams and visions? My personal encounters with God will be unfolded in this book!

How did God convey His instructions to Moses? Why was Joseph known to be a dreamer? The first part of this book revisits these past encounters!

I have written about my episodes last because the first part supports and validates the truth behind the experiences of some notable characters from the ancient days to the early twentieth century, which exhibits the living proof of God's manifestations of His love to His people by giving them His instructions through dreams and visions, regardless of time and age. This inspired me to share my own dreams and visions in order to glorify God's love and faithfulness. I have selected the significant and remarkable episodes, followed by my interpretation and realisation or fruition, which enormously directed my own life and my whole family to the right course of life!

Discover how a seven-year-old-orphan girl was guided by God and the Blessed Mother Mary all the way …

It's time to relax and read these revelations over a cup of coffee or tea!

I sincerely hope and pray for readers' enjoyment and satisfaction, and most of all, that they achieve their awareness and self-discovery of the spiritual gifts present in their lives and use them for God's honour and glory!

Are you ready for the journey?

Lanni Fides

CHAPTER 1

Awareness of My Prophetic Gifts of Dreams and Visions

1. My Spiritual Gifts Unveiled through a Dream

Did I dream last night?

After Stephen and I had our first child, I acquired the habit of recalling whether or not I'd had a dream at night. At times I can vividly remember a dream, right down to the details, like people, colours, and settings. Sometimes I have no recollection at all. You may ask how and why I acquired this habit.

Let me start by giving you a brief introduction of myself. In the last chapter of this book, I'll share about my life's journey. I was born a Catholic and studied in a Catholic school managed by nuns. At a young age, I really loved going to church, attending masses, and novenas, and cleaning the church and arranging flowers for the altar. Attending masses and novenas meant a lot to me. Mass is the highest form of worship. It starts with the Liturgy of the Word, in which the readings and Gospels are proclaimed, and is followed by the sermon from the priest explaining the moral theme of the readings. It culminates in the celebration of the sacrament of the Eucharist, a ceremony commemorating the Last Supper, which Jesus shared with His apostles on their last night together. A novena is a spiritual devotion consisting of the recitation of a set form of prayer for nine successive days, in preparation for a liturgical celebration. An example is a novena to the Sacred Heart of Jesus. The devotees include their personal favours and petitions in the novena. These have been my spiritual food and nourishment, which I believe kept me strong in my faith and trust in the Lord. Through these, I developed a deep relationship with God and His beloved Mother, and my mother too.

When I wake up in the morning, first I say my morning prayers, and then I recall if there was a dream that night. I unknowingly acquired this habit after an absolutely remarkable incident happened in my life. I was five months pregnant with our eldest child, when unexpectedly my obstetrician asked me if I wanted to know the gender of my baby. It was a very quick "no," because I wanted to be surprised and share the joy of waiting with my husband, who was working overseas at that time and sadly wouldn't be with me when I gave birth. He'd miss out on the very first sight of our first child. I completely turned to God and Mother Mary for prayers and petitions. I also prayed hard and hoped to find a lady helper as a support at home after childbirth.

That night, I dreamed of a baby crib adorned with white lace, pink ribbons on the handle, and a pink blanket and tiny white pillows. A woman was busy cleaning the room and putting everything in place!

When I woke up, I was in ecstasy! I prayed my morning prayers with tears of joy, for I knew and felt the message of God, with deep expectant faith, that a baby girl and housemaid were on the way!

"I praise and thank you, Lord!" These were the words I kept repeating the whole day!

Two months before my due date, Aunt Encar visited me and happily mentioned that her long-time friend was looking for work. She'd told her friend that she had a niece (referring to me) who needed a housemaid. That's great news! The next day, I met the housemaid, who was an older woman. I preferred this because I knew she had lots of experiences to share with me. That day was the beginning of a relationship with a loving and reliable companion, which made me feel secure.

The much-awaited time came. I was brought to the hospital and gave birth to a beautiful baby girl. I immediately sent the good news to my husband through a telegram! *Thank you, Lord!*

That was the starting point of my awareness of my prophetic gifts of dreams and visions. My dream of the baby girl and the older woman affirmed that God had spoken to me on that momentous night through that remarkable dream!

From then on, I kept an eye on my dreams and visions and made sure that I wrote them down. I pray and fast when I encounter them, seeking the guidance and wisdom of the Holy Spirit. Then a free-flowing message, or clues on the significance of the dream or vision, will come to me.

> *From the stump of Jesse a shoot will come forth; from his roots a branch will grow and bear fruit. The spirit of the Lord will rest upon him: a spirit of wisdom and understanding, a spirit of counsel and power, a spirit of knowledge and fear of the Lord. (Isaiah 11:1–2)*

Are you experiencing dreams and visions too? If so, then you too are spiritually gifted!

You may be asking, "What's the difference between dreams and visions?"

2. Difference between Dreams and Visions

The main difference between dreams and visions is that the person seeing a vision is completely aware of his or her thoughts, but in dreams the person isn't awake while thoughts, emotions, or even objects unconsciously pass through his or her mind.

Dreams might be forgotten as the person wakes up, or they may stick out vividly. The dreamer may also be able to understand its meaning or interpretation instinctively and spontaneously.

Vision is the ability to see, or plan, something in the future. Visions are generally easily perceived by the visionary. God speaks directly to visionaries, as shown in Numbers 12:8, when God spoke to Moses and said, "To him, I speak face to face, openly, and not in riddles, and he looks at the form of the Lord." In the Bible, the word "vision" is more often used to refer to an encounter with God in which He imparts special revelations and messages.

A vision is an idea, mental image, or an experience in which one can see things that don't exist. It can occur when one's mind is affected powerfully by something, such as deep religious thought. God might be trying to tell us something through that vision.

One kind of vision is called intuitive vision, which is an instinctive feeling in which one is highly sensitive to what others are feeling. They may also be overly protective of their loved ones. Mothers often experience intuitive vision because of their intense love and protection for their own. This is God's gift for their maternal roles and duties; however, this gift is also given to all, regardless of age or gender. It's an ability to know or feel something and then visualise it without any proof; hence, it's called intuitive vision.

Dreams can appear to be very real. Sometimes one wakes up very sad, mad, or scared. The same is true with visions; they can be real in our minds but not a reality.

Both dreams and visions are prophetic. They have the power of foretelling what lies ahead, but they're different in some ways. Visions and dreams have meaning and are subject to interpretation through the guidance and enlightenment of the Holy Spirit. The revelation of the meaning may happen instantly, the next day, or even months and even years into the future.

A vision comes when a person is wide awake and vigilant, while a dream happens when the person is asleep. Peter was awake for his vision of unclean food (Acts 10:9–23); John was awake for his vision recorded in Revelation (Revelation 1:9–11). However, Joseph was asleep and had a dream in which an angel spoke to him about Mary (Matthew 1:20–24).

Some dreams are reflections of a person's subconscious thoughts, which can be past unfulfilled goals, meaningful memories, or the current challenges. Isaiah says, "As when a hungry man dreams he is eating and awakens with an empty stomach" (Isaiah 29:8). And Solomon writes, "For dreams come from over-anxiety and foolish talk from too many words" (Ecclesiastes 5:2).

Some dreams may be part of spiritual warfare in the form of false messages from spiritual enemies. Through Jeremiah, God said this about the "smooth tongued" false prophets:

> *I am against those who base their prophecy on lying dreams, declares the Lord. They tell them and lead my people astray with their lies and pretensions. I did not send them or charge them to speak, and they are of no benefit to this people, declares the Lord. (Jeremiah 23:32)*

God sometimes gives special dreams, such as the experience of Joseph in Genesis 37:5–10, the dream of Solomon in 1 Kings 3:5, and the dreams related to the birth of the Lord Jesus Christ in Matthew 1:2. These dreams provided significant messages that God's servants needed to understand.

Does God speak to us through dreams and visions? The answer is *yes*! The Bible tells us: "After this, I will pour out my Spirit upon all flesh. Your sons and daughters will prophesy, your old men will dream dreams, and your young men will see visions" (Joel 3:1). God actively speaks to us through them, and they can have a scriptural meaning. God uses dreams and visions to bring instructions. The Bible tells us: "In a dream, in a night vision, when deep sleep falls on all, while they slumber in their beds, it is then He opens their ears and gives warning by terrifying them" (Job 33:15–16).

This is why dreams and visions must never be ignored. They are prophetic gifts because they're about the visual aspects of what God is saying. They are the ways God conveys messages to us. God uses dreams and visions to actively communicate His purpose to us, and so they will be revealed, just like the encounters experienced by the biblical characters, prophets, and saints that I have included in the next chapter of this book.

God's special revelation—the Bible—has been completed, and it covers all things about God, His works, and His purposes as revealed to prophets and biblical characters through these divine channels.

I believe that all God's people experience dreams and visions, but they are overlooked due to the busyness of the world. If ever you do encounter this divine medium, pray and take time to listen and hear His voice to clearly understand His instructions and messages. Seek the guidance and enlightenment from the Holy Spirit for the meanings or interpretations of your dreams and visions: "If we live by the Spirit, let us be led by the Spirit" (Galatians 5:25).

For more clarification of the spiritual gifts, the next chapter presents to you the "Gifts of the Holy Spirit."

CHAPTER 2

Gifts of the Holy Spirit

1. What Are the Spiritual Gifts?

What is a spiritual gift? A spiritual gift, or charism, is an extraordinary power given by the Holy Spirit. This is firmly believed by followers to be supernatural graces, which individual Christians need to fulfill the mission of the Church. There are different kinds of gifts but the same Spirit. There are different kinds of service but the same Lord. This truth is clearly written in scripture:

> *There is a diversity of gifts, but the Spirit is the same. There is a diversity of ministries, but the Lord is the same. There is a diversity of works, but the same God works in all. The Spirit reveals his presence in each one with a gift which is also a service. To one is given to speak with wisdom through the Spirit. Another teaches according to the same Spirit. To another is given faith, in which*

> *the Spirit acts; to another the gift of healing by the same Spirit. Another works miracles, another is a prophet, another recognises what comes from the good or evil spirit; another speaks in tongues, and still another interprets what had been said in tongues. And all of this is the work of the one and only Spirit who gives to each one just as he chooses. (1Corinthians 12:4–11)*

"Each one should use whatever gift he has received to serve others, faithfully administering God's grace in its various forms" (1 Peter 4:10).

> *See, the body is one even if formed by many members, but not all of them with the same function. The same with us: though many, we are one body in Christ, depending on one another. Let each of Us, therefore, serve according to our different gifts. He who, by God's gift, is a prophet, let him use it in proportion to his faith. (Romans 12:4–6)*

There are different opinions on the actual numbers of spiritual gifts. God's Word identifies a variety of gifts, which shows His generosity showered on the members of His Church, as long as the gifts are used for His glory. These abilities or gifts, often termed as "charismatic gifts," are administration, knowledge, discernment, healing, prophecy, wisdom, interpretation of tongues, tongues, apostleship, mercy, faith, giving, intercession, missions, miracles, teaching, evangelism, hospitality, service, music, encouragement, pastoring, and leadership.

If you're a Christian touched by the power of the Holy Spirit, never doubt that you have some of these charismatic gifts. If at this stage you're not aware which one, fervently pray that the Holy Spirit will reveal it to you. Seek God's guidance and trust His mysterious ways in giving you these gifts. The Holy Spirit gives them freely to those who are willing to receive them. Ask for them and use them out of love.

"May God, the source of hope, fill you with joy and peace in your faith, so that your hope may increase greatly by the power of the Holy Spirit" (Romans 15:13).

You may ask: How will I receive these gifts?

2. How to Receive the Spiritual Gifts

"Cleanliness is next to Godliness" has been a popular saying since time immemorial; it's very ancient and beyond memory! In order to receive the gifts of the Holy Spirit, you must be willing to open your heart and soul to God. Secondly, you must be ready to repent and ask forgiveness for the wrongs you've done and the sins you've committed. This is the stage of cleansing and clearing out your dirt and baggage. Thirdly, you need to let the Holy Spirit enter and dwell in your heart, mind, and soul, and then you live a clean and holy life. Erase bad or evil thoughts, speak kind and gentle words, and give a helping hand and show generosity to others. Develop a deep relationship with God; be prayerful and a practising good Christian. Always seek the guidance of the Holy Spirit in all your endeavours.

Peter, in his Pentecost sermon, explained how to receive the spiritual gifts. He said, "Each of you must repent and be baptised in the name of Jesus Christ, so that your sins may be forgiven. Then you will receive the gift of the Holy Spirit" (Acts 2:38).

To be filled and led by the Spirit of God doesn't require any great spiritual work on our part, or a specific prayer before the Holy Spirit enters into us. It comes through the good news of Christ's innocent sufferings and death for the sins of the world. God graciously calls us sinners to turn from our sins and toward Christ Jesus for forgiveness and life everlasting (2Thessalonians 2:13–14).

In the death and resurrection of Jesus, Paul had the assurance that God does effect a change in our relationship with Him, and it comes only by accepting Jesus in faith that people can be made righteous by God (Romans 3:24–26). When by the grace of God we believe this and trust in Christ as our Saviour, being baptised into His name and according to His command for the remission of our sins (Matthew 28:19), we receive the gifts of the Holy Spirit. He takes up residence in our hearts, teaches us of Jesus from God's Word, and strengthens and keeps us in the true and saving faith (John 14:16–18, 23–28, 16:13–15).

"Since God began such a good work in you, I am certain that He will complete it on the day of Christ Jesus" (Philippians 1:6). Firmly believe that the gifts of the Holy Spirit dwell in you and need to be awakened through constant prayers and strong connection with God. Use and share these spiritual gifts in order to glorify Him and build up His Church.

The spiritual gifts of dreams and visions fall under the gifts of prophecy and wisdom. Everything great that has ever been accomplished was completed through vision, which will be proven in the following chapters. They will reveal some remarkable, significant, spiritually gifted characters who wholeheartedly used their gifts to edify and build up God's Church.

Keep and use the gifts, for these are freely given to you by God for a reason. He has distinctly chosen you, so use these gifts for love and out of love for the greater glory of God:

> *"All of us, whether Jews or Greeks, slaves or free, have been baptised in one Spirit to form one body and all of us have been given to drink from the one Spirit" (1 Corinthians 12:13).*

3. Use Your Spiritual Gifts for God's Glory

Some people are aware that they have spiritual gifts but prefer to ignore them. It's challenging for them because of the many expectations to live in holiness. But this is the right way to be!

This is the perfect way to be closer to God and develop an intense relationship with Him—using one's gifts is praising, honouring, and glorifying our Lord God Almighty! God will particularly use the gifts of dreams and visions to contact us. He may also reach us through another person, an image, a phrase, or a feeling. If you have a repeating dream, you may think it's not important, but it might leave a lingering feeling in your heart. Don't ignore these feelings; instead, analyse them, because they contain a message from God.

Pay attention to the symbolism and meaning in your dreams. God often uses symbolism to give you the answers you seek. That's why it's advisable to write down even the most insignificant part of your dreams, because that one part could be the key to unlocking what the dream means and what God is trying to tell you.

People often ignore their gifts out of the fear of making mistakes or giving the incorrect interpretation of dreams and visions. Remember, that's pride, and it's a sin! One has to be strong in their faith that God is with them and will guide them and not abandon them. Here are some biblical passages showing that God is always with us:

"I will teach you. I will show you the way to follow. I will watch over you and give you counsel" (Psalm 32:8).

"For the Lord gives wisdom, and from His mouth come knowledge and insight" (Proverbs 2:6).

"The Lord makes firm a man's steps when he takes delight in him. They may stumble, but they will not fall, for the Lord holds them by the hand" (Psalm 37:23–24).

"If any of you is lacking in wisdom, let him ask God who gives it to everyone generously and ungrudgingly, and it will be given to him. But he should ask with faith, not doubting, for he who doubts is like a wave driven and tossed by the wind on the sea" (James 1:5–6).

"Have no fear, for I am with you; be not dismayed, for I am your God. I will give you strength, and bring you help, I will uphold you with my right hand of justice" (Isaiah 41:10).

So there is nothing to fear!

Dreams and visions are messages from God. In the Old Testament alone there are more than 120 mentions of dreams. They're used to give instructions directly from God and to prophesy about the future. Just like Moses' vision of the burning bush from the book of Exodus, where God speaks to him and tells him to lead the Israelites out of Egypt, as well as that memorable moment in our faith's history, again from the vision of burning bush in Mount Sinai, God inscribed the Ten Commandments in two tablets of stone by His own finger through the ball of fire and gave them to Moses for the people to follow these laws as a guide for good living and stay away from evil.

Dreams and visions are direct manifestations of the gifts of the Holy Spirit. Through regular prayers and meditations, there is a continual rebirth of our direct connection and unity with God. The passages below clearly affirm God's presence in dreams and visions:

"I slept, but my heart kept vigil" (Song of Songs 5:2).

"I bless the Lord who is my counsellor; even at night my inmost self He guides me" (Psalm 16:7).

"Probe my heart, search me at night, test me by fire, and you will find no wickedness in me" (Psalm 17:3).

"Do not neglect the spiritual gift conferred on you with prophetic words when the elders laid their hands upon you. Let these be your concern; devote yourself to them, so that your progress may be seen by all" (1 Timothy 4:14–15).

Let go and let God! Let the Holy Spirit freely flow in your life!

Let us now take a journey through chapter 3 and discover the revelations of the significant encounters and remarkable experiences of some biblical characters, prophets, and saints, who experienced the prophetic gifts of dreams and visions, which uplifted and edified God's Church and the strong and solid foundation of Christianity!

CHAPTER 3

Dreams and Visions of Some Biblical Characters, Prophets, and Saints

1. Encounters of Biblical Characters and Saints

a. Patriarch Jacob's Dream of a Ladder

Jacob: 1836–1689 BC (BC means Before Christ)

> *While Jacob was sleeping, he had a dream in which a ladder stood on the earth with its top reaching heaven and on it were angels of God going up and coming down. And the Lord was standing there facing him and said, "I am the Lord, the God of your father Abraham and the God of Isaac. The land on which you sleep, I will give to you and your descendants. Your descendants will be numerous like the dust of the earth and you will spread out to the west and the east, to the north*

and the south. Through you and your descendants all the nations of the earth will be blessed. See, I am with you and I will keep you safe wherever you go. I will bring you back to this land and not leave you until I have done what I promised you." (Genesis 28:12–15)

What Is Jacob's response?

Having received this dream and promise from God, Jacob immediately recognises the power and providence of God, who had made Himself known once again. Jacob woke up from his sleep and said, "Truly the Lord is in this place and I did not know it." He was afraid and said, "How awesome is this place! It is nothing less than a house of God; it is the gate of heaven!" Then Jacob rose early next morning and took the stone he had put under his head and set it up as a memorial and poured oil on the top of it. He named that place Bethel, although before that it was called Luz. Then Jacob made a vow, saying, "If God will be with me and keep me safe during this journey I am making, if He gives me bread to eat and clothes to wear, and if I return safely to my father's house, then the Lord will be my God! This stone which I have set up as a monument will be God's house, and of all that you give me I will give back a tenth." (Genesis 28:16–22)

Reflections

God spoke with Jacob through this dream of a ladder during his flight from his twin brother, Esau, after tricking Esau into giving him his birthright in the family line of inheritance. But God wanted Jacob to know that he was God's chosen heir to fulfill God's promise to Abraham to multiply his descendants into a great nation that God would call His own. Jacob became conscious of his responsibility, for he knew he would be accountable to God, who had chosen him. He expressed this by building an altar and taking a vow.

The ladder represented the connection between God and humanity. It demonstrated that God, who created the universe, desires an intimate relationship with His creation, especially people. It became the symbol of communion with God, and later Jesus would metaphorically declare that He is the "true ladder" of communion with God, as written in John 1:51: "Truly, I say to you, you will see the heavens opened and the angels of God ascending and descending upon the Son of Man." By this saying, Jesus is inviting all of us to a higher vision to see Him as the new Bethel, the house of God, the person in whom there is the abundance of divine presence and guidance to follow God's plan and will for us.

b. Saint Joseph's Four Dreams

Joseph: c.1–c. 100 (c. stands for "circa," the Latin word for "around" or "approximately")

Saint Joseph was chosen to be the husband of Mary. The means of communication God used to speak to him was through dreams. He heard God's messages and instructions in his sleep.

First Dream: An angel appeared in Joseph's dream, telling him about Mary's pregnancy"

> *This is how Jesus Christ was born. Mary his mother was engaged to Joseph; but before they came together as husband and wife, she was found pregnant through the Holy Spirit. Then, her husband made plans to divorce her in all secrecy. For he was an upright man and did not want to disgrace her. While he was pondering over this, an angel of the Lord appeared to him in a dream and said, "Joseph, descendant of David, do not be afraid to take Mary as your wife. She has conceived by the Holy Spirit, and will bear a son." All this happened in order to fulfill what the Lord had said through the prophet: The virgin will conceive and bear a son, and he will be called Emmanuel which means: God with us. (Matthew 1:18–23)*

Second Dream: The angel gave Joseph warning to leave Bethlehem and flee to Egypt.

> *After the wise men had left, an angel of the Lord appeared in a dream to Joseph and said, "Get up, and take the child and his mother and escape into Egypt, and stay there until I tell you. Herod will soon be looking for the child in order to kill him." Joseph got up, and took the child and his mother, and left that night for Egypt; and he stayed there until the death of Herod. In this way, what the Lord had spoken through the prophet was fulfilled: I called my son out of Egypt. (Matthew 2:13–15).*

Third Dream: Herod was dead, so now Joseph and his family were safe to return to Israel.

> *After Herod's death, an angel of the Lord appeared in a dream to Joseph and said, "Get up, and take the child and his mother and go back to the land of Israel, because those who tried to kill the child are dead." So, Joseph got up, took the child and his mother and went to the land of Israel. (Matthew 2:19–21)*

Fourth Dream: Joseph is again warned not to go to Judea.

> *But Joseph heard that Archaelus succeeded his father Herod as king of Judea, he was afraid to go there. He was directed by a dream, and went to the*

> *region of Galilee. There he settled in a town called Nazareth. Thus, what was spoken by the prophets was fulfilled: "He shall be called a Nazarene." (Matthew 2:22–23)*

Reflections

What do we learn from Saint Joseph's dreams? We learned that God can speak, perhaps speaks best, when we are asleep, quiet, and passive. When we're busy, our conscious minds are slowed down, or turned off completely. "I bless the Lord who is my counsellor; even at night guides me" (Psalm 16:7).

A dream sends the Holy Family into Egypt, and another dream brings them back from exile. Joseph's prompt obedience and execution of what the angel commanded him manifests God's control over the events of history. Let Saint Joseph teach us the beauty of quietness and of listening, and let his quiet courage be an example to us all in this frightening moment in history.

> *"Joseph, son of David, do not be afraid," the angel said. Saint Joseph, pray for us. Amen.*

c. Visions of Cornelius and Peter

Cornelius and Peter met c. 33–c. 48 AD (AD stands for Anno Domini, which means the Year of our Lord)

The Vision of Cornelius

There was in Caesarea a man named Cornelius, a centurion in what was called an Italian Cohort. He and his whole household were religious and God-fearing. He gave generously to the people and constantly prayed to God. One afternoon at about three o'clock he had a vision in which he clearly saw an angel of God coming towards him and calling, "Cornelius!"

He stared at the vision in terror and said, "What is it, Lord?"

"Now send men to Joppa and summon a certain man named Simon, a tanner, whose house is beside the sea." As soon as the angel who spoke to him departed, Cornelius called two of his servants and a devout soldier from among those attached to his service, and after having explained everything to them, he sent them to Joppa. (Acts 10:1–8)

The Vision of Peter

The next day, while they were still on their journey and approaching the city, Peter went up to the roof to pray. He became hungry and wish to eat something, and while they were preparing food, he fell into a trance! He saw the heavens opened and an object that looks like a large sheet coming down, and being lowered to the ground by its four corners. In it were all kinds of four-legged animals and reptiles of the earth and birds in the air. Then a voice said to him, "Get up, Peter; kill and eat!"

But Peter replied, "Certainly not, Lord! I have never eaten anything profane or unclean."

And again, a second time the voice spoke, "What God has made clean, you have no right to call profane."

This happened three times and suddenly the sheet was taken up into the sky. While Peter was still doubting over the meaning of the vision he had seen, the messengers sent by Cornelius arrived. They were asking for the house of Simon, a tanner and were now standing at the gate. They called out to inquire whether Simon has a guest name Peter. While Peter was still pondering on the vision, the Spirit spoke to him. "There are three men looking for you. Get up and go downstairs and follow them without hesitation, for I have sent them."

Then Peter went and said to the men, "I am the one you are looking for. What brings you here?"

They answered, "We are coming from Cornelius the centurion. He is an upright and God-fearing man, well respected by all the Jewish people. He has been instructed by a holy angel to summon you to his house, so that he may listen to what you have to say." So, Peter invited them in and put them up for the night.

The next day he went with them and some of the brothers from Joppa accompanied him. The following day, he arrived in Caesarea where Cornelius was expecting them; he called together his relatives and close friends. As Peter was about to enter the house, Cornelius met him, fell at his feet and bowed down. But Peter lifted him up saying, "Stand up, I am only a man." Talking with him, Peter went in and found many people assembled there. Then he said to them, "You know that it is forbidden for Jews to associate with a Gentile or to enter his house. But God has made it clear to me that no one should call any person profane or unclean. So, I came without objection when I was sent for. Now tell me, why you sent for me?"

Cornelius then answered, "Just four days ago at this time, about three in the afternoon, I was

> *praying in my house when a man in shining clothes stood before me. He said to me, 'Cornelius, God has heard your prayers, and remembered your almsgiving. Send someone, therefore, to Joppa and ask for Peter, who is a guest at the house of Simon, a tanner, by the sea.' So, I sent for you at once and you have been kind enough to come. Now we are all here in God's presence to listen to all that the Lord has commanded you to say." (Acts 10:9–33)*

Reflections

Peter's openness of heart and utmost obedience to the mediation of the Holy Spirit, despite of his reluctancy in the beginning, had paved way to a new horizon of peacebuilding and unity between the Jews and the Gentiles. Through the Holy Spirit, he was enlightened to the truth that God made it clear that no one should call any person unclean. Cornelius, on the other hand, greatly contributed to this unity, being a God-fearing man and a believer of the One True God and followed the message of God to send for Peter. What a great combination of two chosen leaders who manifested their prompt obedience to their call and intense love of God. The baptism of Cornelius and his people resulted to the unification of two races.

Once again, the visions encountered by Peter and Cornelius, with their profound love of God, resulted to the significant changes in the Christendom world, which opened its door to anyone who wants to be baptised and becomes a believer of Christ Jesus, our Saviour and Redeemer.

This certainly reminded me of the vision of St John XXIII, who in 1959 called all the world's Catholic bishops to Rome with the aim of modernising the Church, like allowing other languages in Masses for the sake of other faiths and eventually called the Second Vatican Council, which shocked the Roman Catholic world. Through the intervention of the Holy Spirit, just like the visions of Cornelius and Peter, everything was made possible. Vatican II was created, in which the Catholic Church opened its doors and windows to a new relationship with other Christian churches and other religions, with a recognition that there was possible salvation outside the Catholic Church.

Indeed, in both visions of these notable saints manifested God's power that everything is possible with Him. A humble response to the call is all what it takes. "For human beings this is impossible, but for God all things are possible." (Matthew 19:26)

d. Dream of Saint Francis of Assisi: Battlefield's Glory

Saint Francis of Assisi: 1181–1220 AD

Saint Francis, as a young man had a deep passion to be a knight, for he believed that he finds glory in the battlefield. Through his persistence, he joined the Assisi army of the nearby city of Perugia. Not long after, his army lost and he spent time of depression and desolation in a prison of Perugia. He sadly returned home, but still kept his passion of becoming a knight. He ignored the harsh words of his father and planned to move on for the next step towards knighthood. That night he dreamed, that he was in a majestic palace surrounded with walls of banners and military shields. He interpreted this dream as 'his glory in the battlefield.'

Francis' Dream at Spoleto

No one can stop young Francis, so he bought a horse and armour and travelled towards Rome. He stopped at Spoleto for the night and right here, was the start of remarkable changes in his life. God spoke to him in his dream! God asked him, "Who are you serving, the Master or the servant?" Francis quickly answered, "The Master." But God told him that he was obeying the servant and not the Master. So, Francis asked God what to do. God commanded him to go home and there he will find his mission.

Revelation of Francis' Dream

Francis' life turned around because of his encounter with God at Spoleto. In his constant prayers, he started to feel God's love and faithfulness. This was the point in his life when he learned to love and give service to the poor and even embraced a leper he met on the road. At the chapel of San Damiano, he heard words of Jesus asking him to fix His church, for it badly needed repairs. He literally took the meaning of what Jesus said, so took fabric from his father's shop, who was a merchant and sold it in order to produce money to repair the church. His father was so enraged of this act of theft and called Francis as a madman. He took him to the bishop and told everything of what happened. The bishop asked Francis to return the money, for God would give everything he needed for his mission. So then Francis returned the money and everything that his father gave him including his clothes he was wearing at that time, and just left himself a thin shirt. He declared in front of the crowd that he has no more father except Our Father in Heaven.

From that day onwards, Francis started his mission faithfully obeying God's call. He restored abandoned and dilapidated churches. One significant tiny church, which he rebuilt was St Mary of the Angels, which eventually became the home of the whole Franciscan family. He founded later on, communities of men and women: the men's Order of Friars Minor, the women's Order of St Clare, and the Third Order of St Francis, living the life of humility, poverty and love for the disadvantaged and impoverished.

Reflections

Without retelling the whole story of St Francis, we know that his original dream was fulfilled in wonderful ways. God manifested His plan for St. Francis, which was different from his. In short, Francis became an acclaimed knight of Christ and "the messenger of the Great King."

The photo of the sad saint on a horse now stands before a magnificent basilica where thousands and thousands come each week to honour one of the world's great saints and to pray at his tomb. His life was a clear example of humanity's weakness in listening to God's voice, but through divine intervention and strong faith and a solid connection with God, he later on finds the right path toward God's plan.

e. Saint Teresa of Calcutta's Early Visions

Saint Teresa of Calcutta: 1910–1997

Saint Teresa of Calcutta was an Albanian-Indian Roman Catholic nun and missionary. She was born on August 26, 1910 in Skopje, then part of the Kosovo Vilayet of the Ottoman Empire. She devoted her life to caring for the sick and poor. She was a frail nun who became the symbol of selfless charity.

Teresa was the founder and Superior General of the Missionaries of Charity. Later in her life, she was forced to give up her life's work helping the sick and dying because of ill health. She died on September 5, 1997.

God's Call on the Train: 1928–1948

Mother Teresa was a nun and teacher at the Sisters of Loreto in India. On a train journey, she heard the voice of God telling her to leave and go to the slums of Calcutta and bring to Him the poor, the sick, the dying, and the little street children. God told her that He wanted an Indian Missionary Sisters of Charity to do this mission for Him. She didn't listen to His voice, in spite of His constant call on her train journeys. She even disputed the voice she heard, and after receiving Holy Communion, she knelt and begged God to find someone else. She knew the hardship, difficulty, and even mockery she would endure once she revealed this calling to her superiors. God told her that He was deeply hurt to see the poorest of the poor suffering. She was touched by God's utmost love for the poor, so she mentioned this voice and conversations with God to her superior, Archbishop Perier. As expected, there were many questions and proceedings involved, so the process took months.

Divine Visions of Jesus and Mary

Mother Teresa persistently wrote letters to Archbishop Perier, asking about the progress of her request to leave the convent and go into the slums and start her mission. In one of her letters, she revealed her divine visions of Jesus and Mary, as well as conversations she'd had with them. She wrote that she saw Jesus on the cross, Mary at a little distance from the cross, and herself as a little child. Again, He asked her to take care of the poor and bring them to Him. Mary repeated her son's words, and Mother Teresa humbly replied that she was ready to abide and just waiting for permission from the Pope.

Upon receiving Mother Teresa's letter about the visions of Jesus and Mary, the Archbishop presented it to all the priests and bishops under his jurisdiction. Not so long after, they stated that Mother Teresa's visions were legitimate and genuine. Her request was urgently sent to the Pope.

Start of the Mission

Pope Pius XII granted permission for Mother Teresa to leave the Loreto Sisters, just before her thirty-eighth birthday in 1948. She was required to keep her vows of poverty, chastity, and obedience and be under the authority of Archbishop Perier. Upon hearing this good news, she immediately asked her superior if she could go out that very day. Without wasting a minute, she stepped out of the convent, dressed in her simple white sari and with few rupees in her pocket.

Mother Teresa enthusiastically started her mission by studying short courses on basic medicine, teaching the poor street children, and meeting up with the people in the slums of Calcutta. Some former students joined her in this mission with the help of the Little Sisters of the Poor, who warmly invited her to live with them in the convent.

By 1950, this unofficial group of women was recognized by the Church as a newly found religious order, named The Missionaries of Charity.

Reflections

When Jesus Christ was teaching His disciples how to best show their love for Him, He said, "Truly, I say to you, whenever you did this to one of the least of my brothers, you did it to me" (Matthew 25:40).

There was a heroic side of this small statured woman with the biggest heart that was revealed only after her death. It had been hidden from all eyes, even from those closest to her. Truly she was a perfect model of humility who showed no interest in recognitions and praises. After her death, all eyes were focused on her as a remarkable woman of great faith and profound love for the poor and the sick.

Mother Teresa was canonized by Pope Francis on September 4, 2016 and named her Saint Teresa of Calcutta, a humble champion to the poorest of the poor. Saint Teresa of Calcutta is considered one of the twentieth century's greatest humanitarians, who intensely listened to and obeyed the visions and calling of God.

2. Encounters of Prophets: Visions of God

a. Moses and Aaron, Nadab and Abihu, and Seventy Elders of Israel

Moses' Time: approximately Anno Mundi 2666 (Anno Mundi means the year after creation)

> *Then Moses went up with Aaron, Nadab, Abihu and the seventy elders of Israel. They saw the God of Israel. Under His feet, there was what seemed*

> *like a pavement of sapphire, clear as the sky itself. But he did not let his hand over power these noblemen from the sons of Israel, they looked on God and lived to eat and drink. The Lord said to Moses, "Come up to me on the mountain and stay there. I will give you the slabs of stone, the law and the commandment which I have written for their instructions." (Exodus 24:9–12)*

Instructions about the Sanctuary

> *The Lord spoke to Moses and said, "Tell the sons of Israel to set aside a contribution for Me; you shall accept this contribution from every man who gives from the heart. These things you shall accept from them are these: gold, silver, and bronze, purple cloth of violet shade and red, crimson cloth, fine linen, goats' hair, rams' skins dyed red, fine leather, acacia wood, oil for the lamps, spices for the chrism, and for the fragrant incense; precious stones and gems to be set in priestly vestments and breast piece. For you must build me a sanctuary so that I may dwell among them, and you shall make this Tabernacle and its furnishings following exactly the pattern I shall show you." (Exodus 25:2–9)*

Reflections

God loves Moses, and Moses in turn loves God. So God gave Moses direct and clear instructions on what He wanted: how His people should pray to Him, in what holy dwelling His people would find Him, and what the most sacred Tabernacle was to be made of and what it should look like in order to honour Him and pay homage to Almighty God.

Moses is regarded as one of the greatest prophets, or even the greatest of all. As written in the biblical history, he was the little Hebrew baby boy in a reed basket found in the Nile River by the Pharoah's daughter. At that time, there was an order to kill all newborn Hebrew males to restrict the growth of their race. He was named Moses and raised in the Egyptian court. During his education, he discovered his true origin. When he went to visit his people, he witnessed their sufferings under the Egyptians. This began his strong connection with Yahweh, which led him to live with his own people and be exiled. His profound obedience to Yahweh's command led to the deliverance of the Hebrews. He recognised his weaknesses, but he was empowered by Yahweh, so Moses made history liberating the Hebrews from slavery, which led to the birth of a new nation—Israel.

This is a splendid image of a trusting and loving Master to an ever-faithful and obedient servant, with a very deep and intense relationship to His Lord and Master!

b. Isaiah Saw the Lord Sitting upon a Throne

Isaiah: c. eighth century BC

In the year that King Uzziah died, I saw the Lord seated on a throne, high and exalted; the train of His robe filled the temple. Above Him were seraphs, each with six wings: two is to cover the face, cover the feet, and two to fly with. They were calling to one another: "Holy, holy, holy is the Lord of hosts. All the earth is filled with His glory!"

At the sound of their voices, the foundations of the threshold shook and the Temple was filled with smoke. I said, "Woe to me! I am doomed! For I am a man of unclean lips living among a people of unclean lips, yet my eyes have seen the King, the Lord of Hosts!"

Then one of the seraphs flew to me; in his hands was a burning coal which he had taken with tongs from the altar. He touched my mouth with it and said, "See, this has touched your lips, your guilt has taken away and your sin is forgiven."

Then I heard the voice of the Lord, "Whom shall I send? Who will go for us?" I answered, "Here I am. Send me!" (Isaiah 6:1–8)

Reflections

Isaiah had a personal encounter with God and marked the beginning and mainstay of his prophetic mission. "The Holy One of Israel" will be one of Isaiah's favourite titles for God. We use this during the Eucharist—"Sanctus."

Confronted with the holiness of God, none of us presume to be clean. Isaiah confesses his own dirtiness and the filth of the people to whom he belongs. Then God, in an almost sacramental way, purifies the prophet so that he is now fit to be His representative.

No one is perfect, except God! We all commit mistakes or wrongdoings. God is merciful. As we ask forgiveness for our sins, with open arms God is there to forgive us. In the Catholic Church, a person goes to the priest to confess his sins and wrongdoings and asks for mercy and forgiveness. The priest, as a representative of God, gives him a blessing and penance. With contrite heart, the person experiences healing through forgiveness from God.

It is God's desire that we remain in holiness and be ready to be His servant when He calls us, just like Isaiah, who became God's faithful servant and prophet once he was purified by God.

c. Ezekiel Saw the Vision of Heaven

Ezekiel: c. 622–c. 570 BC

> *Above it was a throne resembling a sapphire and high above on his throne was a figure similar to that*

of a man. Then I saw that from what appeared to be his waist upward he looked like glowing bronze, as if full of fire; and from what appeared to be his waist downward he looked like fire; and brilliant light surrounded him. The surrounding light was like a rainbow in the clouds after a day of rain. This vision was the likeness of the Lord's Glory! On seeing it, I fell on my face and then I heard a voice of one speaking. (Ezekiel 1:26–28)

Ezekiel Receives His Mission

He said to me, "Son of man, stand up for I am about to speak to you." A spirit came upon me as He spoke and kept me standing and then I heard Him speak. He said, "Son of man, I am sending you to the Israelites, to a people who have rebelled against me; they and their fathers have been in revolt against me to this day. Now I am sending you to these defiant and stubborn people to tell them, 'The Lord God says this.' So, whether they listen or not, this set of rebels will know there is a prophet among them. But, you, son of man, do not fear them, or what they say, for they will be as thorns for you and you will be sitting on a nest of scorpions. Do not be afraid of their words nor be dismayed at their looks, for they are a rebellious house. Tell them what I say whether they choose to listen or not, for they are a tribe of rebels. Listen then, Son of man, to what I say and do not be a rebel among rebels. Open your mouth and take in what I am about to give you." Then I looked, and a hand stretched out to me, holding a scroll. He unrolled it before me; on both sides of it were written lamentations, groaning and woes. (Ezekiel 2:1–9)

Then He said to me, "Son of man, eat what is given to you. Eat this scroll and then go; speak to the people of Israel." I opened my mouth and He gave me the scroll to eat; then He said to me, "Son of man, eat and fill yourself with this scroll that I am giving you." I ate it and it tasted as sweet as honey. He then said, "Son of man, go to the house of Israel and speak to them my words. Indeed, it is not a people with a difficult foreign language to whom you are sent; it is to the people of Israel. It is not to the many nations with difficult and obscure languages which you cannot understand that I am sending you, if I sent you to them, they would listen to you. But the Israelites will not listen to you because they are not willing to listen to me; all of them are defiant and stubborn of heart. See I am making you as unyielding as they are and as obstinate as they are. I am making your forehead as hard as a diamond and harder than flint; so, you shall not fear or tremble because of this set of rebels." He then said to me, "Son of man, listen carefully and take to heart all I say to you, and then go to the exiles, your fellow countrymen, speak to them and tell them, 'This is what the Lord God says' whether they listen or not."

Then the Spirit lifted me up, and behind me I heard a loud rumbling sound, "Blessed be the Glory of the Lord in his dwelling place!" And I heard the sound of the wings of the living creatures brushing against each other, and at the same time the sound of the wheels, a great vibrating sound. Then the Spirit lifted me up and carried me off, and I went in bitterness and anger, for the hand of the Lord was heavy on me. I came to Tel Abib, to the exiles living by the river of Chebar and I stayed there seven days them, in a state of consternation. (Ezekiel 3:1–15)

Reflections

Ezekiel is a prophet chosen by God to go to the rebels, known for their hard headedness and stubbornness. But with the divine power of God, Ezekiel faithfully obeyed with the trust in the Lord. God told him to internalise and absorb the word of God and be not afraid to speak before the exiles and not be discouraged if they rejected or ignored what he told them. Ezekiel went with anxiety in his heart, but ready to face whatever the consequences would be.

God called Ezekiel as 'Son of man' which just simply means a man, different from God. Being a chosen prophet, he was commissioned by God to restore Israel. With the blessings and graces from God, Ezekiel later on became the comforter and consoler of the exiles, and led them to return to their homeland. What a remarkable and notable man of God, and a chosen prophet favoured and trusted by God!

d. Stephen Looked up into Heaven and Saw God's Glory

Stephen: 5–34 AD

> *Stephen boldly spoke to the Jewish people, he said, "You are stubborn people, uncircumcised in hearts and ears, you are always resisting the Holy Spirit, just as your fathers did. Was there a prophet whom your fathers did not persecute? They killed those who foretold the coming of the Just One whom you have now betrayed and murdered, you who received the Law through the angels but did not observe it." When the Jewish people heard these things, they were enraged and they gnashed their teeth at Stephen. But Stephen, full of the Holy Spirit, gazed into heaven and saw the glory of God and Jesus at God's right hand. "Look!" he said, "I*

see the heavens opened and the Son of Man standing at the right hand of God." But they shouted and covered their ears with their hands, and rushed together upon him. They brought him out of the city and stoned him. The witnesses laid down their garments at the feet of a young man named Saul. (The witness Saul "after his conversion" becomes Paul.) As they were stoning him, Stephen prayed, "Lord Jesus, receive my spirit." Then he knelt down and said in a loud voice, "Lord, do not hold this sin against them." And when he had said this, he fell asleep." (Acts 7:51–60)

Reflections

Stephen was the first martyr among the apostles of Jesus Christ. Fearlessly, he boldly and openly called the Jews as 'stubborn people' to the point that they got enraged with him and stoned him to death. But for Stephen, dying for Christ is reaching the glory of heaven as he saw it when he looked up the sky---God's glory with Jesus on His right hand! That was more than enough to give his own life. This was witnessed by Saul, one of the persecutors of Jesus Christ, who later on was converted and called Paul by God. He heard Stephen's words of forgiveness to his murderers and humbly followed what Jesus did as he forgave his persecutors.

Stephen's martyrdom paved the way to the addition of another apostle, who was considered one of the greatest apostles of Jesus in the Apostolic Age. He witnessed the strong conviction of Stephen's faith, which opened his mind and heart that Jesus is truly the Son of God and the Messiah.

e. John Was in the Spirit; One Sat on the Throne Set in Heaven

Saint John the Apostle: c. 6–c. 100 AD

The Heavenly Court

After this I had another vision and saw an open door in heaven. And the voice which I had first heard speaking to me like a trumpet said, "Come up here, and I will show you what will take place hereafter." Immediately the Spirit seized me. There, in heaven, was a throne and on the throne sat one whose appearance looked like jasper and camelian, and around the throne was a rainbow resembling an emerald.

> *In a circle around the throne were twenty-four thrones and seated on these were twenty-four elders, dressed in white clothes, with golden crowns on their heads. From the throne came forth flashes of lightning, rumblings and peals of thunder. Seven flaming torches burned before the throne. These are the seven spirits God. In front of the throne was something that looked like a sea of glass, clear as*

crystal. In the centre and around the throne stood four living creatures, covered with eyes in front and behind. The first living creature was like a lion, the second like an ox, the third had the lace like that of a human being, and the fourth looked like a flying eagle. Each of the four living creatures had six wings covered with eyes inside and out. Day and night they sang without ceasing: "Holy, holy, holy is the Lord God the Almighty who was, who is and who is to come." Whenever the living creatures give glory, honour and thanks to the One who sits on the throne, He who lives for ever and ever, the twenty-four elders fall down before him and worship the One who lives forever and ever. They lay down their crowns in front of the throne and say: "Worthy are You, our Lord and God, to receive glory, honour and power! For You have created all things; by Your will they were created and have their existence." (Revelation 4:1–11)

Reflections

John saw the Heavenly Court where God the Father sitting upon His throne surrounded by 24 elders and 4 beasts. The twenty-four elders represent the twelve tribes of Israel and twelve apostles. While the four beasts represent the four evangelist who all honoured God with their written art and literature and most especially the record of Christ's life and teachings in the Gospels of Matthew, Mark, Luke and John.

The vision of John symbolises that God, the creator rules over the whole universe. God's people honour and praise Him with all their might. He is worthy of all praises as King of Kings and Lord of Lords!

We, as His creatures long for the day of seeing God's glory face to face which is called beatific vision and to dwell in this Heavenly Court, which John saw and our eternal home!

Finally, we have reached the last chapter of this book, in which I unfold my journey of encounters with God through dreams and visions! Let me humbly introduce myself before my personal testimonies.

CHAPTER 4

My Personal Encounters with God through Dreams and Visions

1. Self-Introduction

In order to help you gain a better understanding of my beliefs and insights, I'd like to open the book of my life …

Together with my two brothers, "Kuya" Nico and Liam ("Kuya" means elder brother in our dialect), I studied in a Catholic school managed by the Religious of the Virgin Mary Sisters. The religious and moral values we learned from their teachings became the core foundation of our character and personality.

I was almost seven years of age when we lost our mother, whom we called "Nanay" in our dialect. "Tatay" was our word for father. Nanay died of an internal haemorrhage due to a miscarriage. I clearly remember being at Nanay's funeral, surrounded by approximately twenty nuns all dressed in white religious clothing and black veils, as if they were angels protecting us from harm and danger.

"My child, don't be sad; don't be afraid, for you have heavenly Mother Mary, who will look after you. And her Son, Jesus, will be with you always." These were the words of Mother Superior, imprinted in my mind, heart, and soul. They became my comfort and guide from then on.

Kuya Nico, Liam, and I were looked after by our father's sister, Aunt Nina, who was single and lived alone. She lovingly took good care of us, as if we were her own children. She also instilled in us Christian moral values and discipline. I found her to be stricter towards me than my brothers, as she reasoned that I was the only girl and would be the mother of our family later on. It was as if she had the ability to foresee the future.

When I turned eleven, Aunt Nina became seriously ill, and the provincial health department took her away for treatment. She'd acquired a contagious and infectious disease called tuberculosis. Sadly, after two months, Aunt Nina passed away. I took comfort from her words that she repeatedly said to me: "*Be strong and do not fear; God is with you.*" These words again affirmed the uplifting words of Mother Superior at my mother's funeral, which became my mantra and inspiration moving forward, ready to face life's challenges.

True enough, the four years of training from Aunt Nina had prepared me for the role of being the family's housekeeper. But I became a sickly and frail young girl. I wasn't able to cope with the household duties, which led Tatay to remarry. This made me overwhelmingly happy, especially when Nanay Julie, our loving stepmother, gave birth to a beautiful baby girl, Jade. Our family became alive again; our two-storey house, which formerly looked like a haunted house, now was brightened up by the sparkles of chandeliers!

The roller coaster of my life took place again! After two years of peace and happiness with Nanay Julie and baby sister Jade, I was devastated to learn that she'd decided to separate from Tatay due to his infidelity, in spite of my attempt to stop her. I tried to persuade both Tatay and Nanay Julie to see a marriage counsellor to fix their marriage, but Nanay Julie firmly declined, as she was deeply hurt and couldn't trust Tatay ever again. I felt like the sky had fallen on my head, and I couldn't help but burst into tears. I watched them leave the house until they vanished from sight. That was the gloomiest and saddest morning of my life! This aggravated my downhearted feeling, and when I went back inside our empty and lonesome house, with that deafening silence, I couldn't help but weep loudly and cry out my pain and anguish: "Oh Lord God and Mother Mary, help me and comfort me in this unbearable loneliness!"

I slept while holding a rosary and woke up feeling lifted up with peace and comfort in my heart. "With you, Lord God and Mother Mary, I have everything!" These words were engraved within my whole being, which kept me strong and firm!

From then on, at thirteen years of age, I was "fully running the house," with God as my strength and refuge and with the intercession of Mother Mary. At fourteen, I joined the Legion of Mary, a lay Catholic organisation whose members give service to the Church on a voluntary basis, like helping with cleaning the church, arranging flowers for the altars, visiting the sick, and volunteering to do childminding so parents can attend mass. Being an active member of this organisation brought me closer to God and helped me develop a deeper relationship with Jesus. Through my faithfulness to daily mass attendance and prayers, I found myself stronger and firmer when the trials and storms of life came.

I finished my university degree and became a high school teacher, managed by the nuns of the Order of Saint Benedict in a nearby town.

While my spiritual, moral, and emotional being ran smoothly according to God's plan, Kuya Nico's and Liam's sailings were pointing toward the opposite direction in life. They stopped attending school and joined the wrong crowd, until both of them were involved in drugs and alcohol. At that point in my life, I felt I was drowning in so many challenges: brothers troubled with vices and, at the same time, an alcoholic and womanizing father. I needed lots of prayers, patience, and perseverance to get their lives turned around. I didn't give up hope, for I knew that one day God, in His own ways, would show them the right path. This verse gave me inspiration: "Put your hope in the Lord, be strong and courageous; yes, put your hope in the Lord!" (Psalm 27:14).

Meanwhile, I found peace and joy being in the church and with the nuns. It was a complete contrast with the atmosphere at home, for at this stage I could see the family's total immersion into the deep pit of sin and darkness. These shameful scenarios seemed unbearable, to the point that I just left them, like abandoning a sinking ship. I felt overstrained and finally found the courage to seek an audience with the Mother Superior to disclose my desire to join them. She was so delighted to hear my intention, but knowing my family's mess, she said that God wanted me to primarily help and save Tatay and my two brothers, then I could always come back for my vocation. In sadness and despair, I clearly understood what she meant, and I kept the hope in my heart.

With the power of prayers and God's grace, I got up from my bruised and weakened strength and bravely moved on and on! Kuya Nico and I got married and had our own respective families. Liam was still single but living cleaner and in the course of recovery from the pangs of vices. I felt like God had a different plan for me and divinely directed me to a married life. Things went well until a turning point in our lives: Tatay was diagnosed with lung cancer. This put me in a dilemma, because at that time Stephen and I were planning to migrate to Australia with our children. I surrendered everything to God and asked Him to show us the path to His will. God knew what was in my heart: the pain and anguish of being torn between my own family's better future and leaving behind a sick father.

God works in mysterious ways! After six months battling this dreadful disease, Tatay passed away. A year and a half later, our visa to migrate to Australia was approved, which meant that we had the time to celebrate the first death anniversary of our father and to witness the wedding of our youngest brother, Liam. Truly God is in control! Just let go and let God!

In October 1988, Stephen and I together with our three children—Jasmine, age eleven, Matthew, age nine, and Lily, age seven—left our beloved Philippines to start a new life in Australia, and the rest is history.

Now that you know a bit about me, I'm sure you'll easily understand my thoughts and insights.

> *"The Lord bless you and keep you; the Lord make His face to shine upon you and be gracious to you; the Lord lift up His countenance upon you and give you peace" (Numbers 6:24–26).*

Grant, O merciful Father, that your divine Spirit may enlighten, inflame, and purify us to shed light in our souls, and grant us your Spirit of wisdom and understanding so that we might be enlightened with your heavenly inspirations, through Our Lord Jesus Christ, your Son, who with you in the unity of the same Spirit lives and reigns, one God, forever and ever. Amen!

2. Prelude

I discovered my prophetic gifts of dreams and visions when I was twenty-two years of age. With that self-discovery, I was touched and inspired to write about my encounters with the intention of someday sharing them with others and, most importantly, proclaiming God's faithfulness and unconditional love.

God visits us in the night and conveys His message through dreams! As you know, some dreams are just gone and lost when we wake up. Some dreams stick in our minds and truly are unforgettable; the same is true with visions.

I am emphatically repeating how I value my prophetic gifts. When a striking dream or vision occurs, I always grab the opportunity to record it in my journal. Every time meanings, interpretations, and symbols come to me with the guidance of the Holy Spirit, I revisit my journal and update it. The next update comes when the realisation or fruition happens, which varies in time. Sometimes it's the very same day, and sometimes weeks, months, or even years. Praise God! The time has come to share these captured moments with God and glorify His name!

Let me take you now to some of my significant encounters with God through dreams and visions, which dropped a huge impact in our lives as a migrant family. These divine encounters guided us in the right course of life and led our family to the kind of existence or manner of living we are in now… to a beautiful, meaningful and spirit-filled life!

3. Vision: My Baby Falling down the Stairs

August 4, 1978: the date of the vision

At the time of this vision, I was living with Tatay in a historical, two-storey, Spanish-style house with all the wide *capiz* windows and spacious *salas* (Spanish for lounge room), with a porch and a flight of stairs to the second level, where we stayed. Stephen, my hardworking husband, was working overseas at that time. Jasmine, our gorgeous baby, was eleven months old and loved to be on her walker. She enjoyed going around the spacious lounge room, happily playing by herself as the lively music played full blast from Tatay's Quadrosonic stereo, as if she was singing and dancing at the same time.

On the spur of the moment, I felt a sense of discomfort and a sudden anxiety about Jasmine's activity. I wanted to hear the sounds she'd make, but I couldn't due to the blaring sound of the stereo. With my heart throbbing too fast, instinctively *I envisioned a frightening scenario, or an on- going image in my mind of my baby falling on her walker and rolling and rolling down the stairs. Within a split second, I ran toward the door while simultaneously shouting, "My baby! Check on her; the door might be open, and she might go to the porch where the stairs are!"* I hadn't even reached the door when I heard the sound of the walker falling down the stairs to the ground as I called all the angels and Saints to hold my baby to safety! As I looked down on the ground, I saw Jasmine steadily standing and holding on to her walker. She looked at me with a delightful smile, as if saying, "That was a wonderful ride!" She was waving a toy, as if nothing had happened! Oh my Lord God, all angels and Saints, thank you for holding my baby on the palms of your hands!

Interpretation and Realisation

The fact that women carry their children inside their own bodies for nine months, being one physical, mental, and emotional being, might explain a mother's intuition. It's a natural instinct for many mothers to sense when their child is in danger, or to pick out their child's cry from within a group of other children, which is true even of animals. One good example is the world of penguins. Once the mother or father returns from their fishing trips, they can recognise their baby penguin's cry from a distance.

Mothers are highly intuitive because of the great bond they have with their children, and certainly the love for their children comes closest to the definition of divine love. It's the purity and strength of this affection that allows her into the power of the Holy Spirit. Mothers become highly spirited human beings through constant prayer, and in turn they're empowered by God and gifted with wisdom and knowledge. They become almost spiritual beings through the deep love and sense of protection they feel for their children. A mother's intuition is perhaps just a small part of that entire spiritual experience of motherhood.

What I encountered absolutely affirms the existence of intuitive vision, commonly present in all of us but not used to the fullest due to things like loss of interest, selfish motivations, and absence of a spiritual life. The key factors to make use of intuitive vision include the presence of intense love, humility, faithfulness to prayer, and the Holy Spirit in one's life.

> *"He will cover you with His pinions, and give you refuge under His wings; His faithfulness will be your shield" (Psalm 91:4).*

4. Dream: Two Intertwined Hearts in Rainbow Colours

a. Prelude

March 8, 1986: On this day, I saw a perfect rainbow

Illustrated by Raphael

Stephen's sister, Leni, and her husband visited Manila, Philippines after five years of being Australian citizens, bringing with them several sponsorship forms that they joyfully shared with all of the brothers and sisters who were qualified to apply as migrants. As a big family in the Philippines, we regarded this as great blessing and opportunity for our better future. It was as if we had won the lottery!

Stephen and I took one form, prepared all necessary documents, and then travelled to Manila to submit the application form at the Australian Embassy. Before going to the Embassy, we attended mass at Quiapo Church and fervently prayed for God's blessings and graces for the success of this intention.

Travelling back to the province, I was praying the Rosary in silence when I saw a perfect rainbow! I was seated in the front seat on the aisle side, so the road was clearly visible to me. It was a bright, sunny afternoon, and this rainbow was a magnificently perfect dome shape, from end to end in bright colours. We were travelling towards it, getting closer and closer and closer! That was the first time in my life I saw such a perfect and complete rainbow!

Interpretation and Realisation of the Perfect Rainbow Sign

I regard the rainbow as a symbol or a sign of great hope for an aspiration or desire. God sends His message of hope, saying, "Be still, know that I am your God. I am supreme among the nations, exalted over the earth!" (Psalm 46:10). What a great relief and assurance that God knows and understands my anxieties and worries. It also symbolises peace and eternal life.

As I shared in the beginning, this was the same time when Tatay was diagnosed with lung cancer. God gave me the message that He is in control and not to worry. He knew that I was in a dilemma—to leave for my own family's better future or to stay and look after my very sick father.

As I was the only grown-up girl in the family, Tatay had completely depended on me since separating from his second wife, Nanay Julie. I couldn't envisage myself leaving him while he was very ill. The message from the perfect rainbow kept my nerves together in this difficult situation.

The Holy Spirit prompted me to complete one more mission. After Nanay Julie left Tatay, their communication had totally stopped. But I had regularly visited her and my step-sister, Jade. I actually convinced Tatay to let Jade stay with us on the weekends, which made me extremely happy. Because of this arrangement, Jade and I established a strong bond of love, which has flourished day by day up to the present time; we're like real sisters. The doctor said that Tatay's health had quickly deteriorated. I heard the Holy Spirit's voice telling me to act fast on this mission of reconciliation: first with God, and secondly with Nanay Julie. Through God's power and grace, I victoriously got our parish priest, Father Raul, to visit Tatay and give him the sacraments of confession and extreme unction.

After these holy and sacred ceremonies, Nanay Julie accepted my invitation to visit Tatay and reconcile. They asked each other's forgiveness and both found peace and love again through this divinely inspired reconciliation and reunification. I was so ecstatic and filled with the spirits of love, joy, and peace!

True to God's promise, He controlled everything. Tatay rested in His bosom, our visa to Australia was approved, and my youngest brother, Liam, finally settled down and got married! Again, I felt God's love, His mysterious ways, and divine will. I praise and thank you, Lord!

March 8, 1986: date of the dream

Illustrated by Maya

Because of my overwhelming happiness over what I'd clearly seen that day, that night I had a dream about a rainbow, but it was different! *In this dream, I was in the elementary school on the second floor of the school convent, which had the best panoramic view of the town. Due to the clear visibility of the horizons, it was like reaching up to the heavens. Amazingly, I saw in the sky two intertwined hearts—not only brightly coloured in red but with the rest of the rainbow colours!*

As I woke up that morning, the sign of the rainbow during the day and the dream at night were both clear and transparent to me. Through the guidance and enlightenment of the Holy Spirit, I understood the meanings and messages of God for both.

Interpretation and Realisation

My husband, Stephen, and I were both active in our parish church services. We were both devoted to serving in recollections and retreats, with the aim of helping others to know God, be closer to Him, and deeply understand our faith. These are means of attaining spiritual growth and enrichment given by the parishes, schools, and Catholic groups. A recollection provides participants with teachings about Christian life, concentrating on the presence of God. It may run half a day, one full day, or overnight to a second day. A retreat gives the participants the opportunity for more time spent in prayer and contemplation to hear clearly God's call and to seek His healing grace, which leads to spiritual renewal. It may cover several days or even weeks.

In what way did we give our service here? We invited participants within the parishes and schools to attend and helped in raising funds to cover the cost, as they are provided free to people. When asked, we shared our experiences in our spiritual journey. It was a great honour and privilege to serve the Lord in any way we could!

In this dream, God gave us a message as a couple—to continue evangelising and spreading the good news of God's unconditional love once we set foot in our second home country, Australia. As a family, we were commissioned to bring souls to God so that they too could have a closer relationship with Him. I clearly saw the divine plan of God for me and my family—why I hadn't been accepted by the Mother Superior when I disclosed my sincere intention of being a nun.

In October 1988, we arrived in Australia, enthusiastically carrying the mission in our hearts. God allowed us to settle down first, through His divine providence and the guidance of the Holy Spirit. We both easily found a decent job, acquired a humble dwelling and roof over our heads, and settled the kids in school.

After three years, we were invited to join a movement called Couples for Christ, a Catholic Charismatic family movement with the main mission of "Families renewing the Face of the Earth." Actually, this was our third invitation, because at the time of the first two invitations, we weren't ready, as we were adjusting and settling into the way of life here in Australia. The whole family worked hard together as a team, even on weekends, just to earn extra money to pay off our debts in the

Philippines. We only borrowed money from a "loan shark," at high interest, to cover our airfare. This extra work during the weekends thankfully cleared us of those debts after three years. Now we were ready to roll! I praise and thank you, Lord God Almighty!

Lo and behold, this was what we were looking for, especially for our children, who were almost in their teenage years. We desperately wanted them to be with teenagers of the same faith. So we joined this community in October 1991 and have been active members up to the present time.

Let me share this very clear and affirming manifestation of God's power shown in this dream! After two years as members of the community, we were assigned to travel to Couples for Christ Canberra, in order to share with the members there our own experiences as an active family in service. They particularly wanted to hear from our three teenagers, who were all members of Youth for Christ, a youth ministry under the umbrella of Couples for Christ. Later on, all stepped up as leaders in this ministry.

The brothers and sisters in Canberra warmly welcomed us, but what significantly struck me was seeing a painting of *two intertwined hearts* on the wall. It gave me shivers through my whole body. I felt like I was about to faint with the shock of joy as tears rolled down my cheeks! At the same time, Lily, our youngest daughter, loudly exclaimed, "Look, Mum, your dream!" She remembered that dream too! She was only four years of age when I told her my dream, and when she came back from her pre-school, she eagerly showed me her art interpretation of the dream. It was similar to this painting we were now looking at! That was indeed amazing!

This unforgettable family experience showed us that we were on the right path and following God's plan for us. We shared these experiences with the Canberra members, specifically the beauty and value of being together as one family in faith and action. Inspired and touched by the Holy Spirit, the group eagerly started their Youth Ministry program. God guided us all along and never left us as we followed the flow of the river towards His Kingdom through the guidance of the Holy Spirit.

As I write this book, our three children have their own careers, humble dwellings, and families with two children each, a boy and a girl, making us proud grandparents to three handsome boys and three beautiful girls. Jasmine married Jeremiah and had Jean and Jermaine. Matthew married Raelyn and had Raphael and Mae, and Lily married Marty and had Christopher and Maya.

This is the perfect meaning of the *two-hearts intertwined in rainbow colours ... as couples intertwined with the love for Christ and families in the Holy Spirit, renewing the face of the earth!* Thank you, oh Lord God Almighty, for showing us your way and allowing us to be your instruments as a family to proclaim the good news! Amen!

"Trust in the Lord with all your heart; do not rely on your own insight. Let His presence pervade all your ways, and He will make your path smooth" (Proverbs 3:5–6).

5. Dream: A Girl Flown up in the Sky by Hundreds of Colourful Balloons

August 10, 2001: the date of the dream

Illustrated by Mae

Indeed! God is always true to His promise of divine providence and protection: "Be valiant and strong, do not fear or tremble before them, for the Lord, your God, is with you; He will not leave you or abandon you." (Deuteronomy 31:6).

Three months after our arrival in Australia, God blessed us with our humble dwelling in January 1989. It was a quiet suburban area, close to shops, schools, and church. Most of all, it was in a safe location, being on a battle axe, with plenty of space at the back for the kids to play. The whole family loved the place, to the point that Stephen and I were determined to live there until our retirement. A battle axe is a large, wide block of land subdivided into two properties, one at the front and one at the back. The block at the back has its own access to the street through a narrow driveway, which gives the land an L-shape, like a battle axe. The handle is the narrow entrance-driveway leading to the head of the axe, the main property. Stephen and I purposely chose this kind of block for the safety and security of the kids.

After thirteen years of living in this quiet neighbourhood, the kids had grown older and we thought of building something like a teenagers' retreat at the back. In the future, it could be converted into a granny's flat for us when we retire, due to the space in the back yard. But we were frustrated to learn that there was a stormwater easement in the middle of the yard! No wonder our driveway was always flooded during heavy rains. It was a struggle every time this happened, because that meant mud and dirt everywhere.

We conducted a lot of research to determine if it was still advisable to build, in spite of the storm water easement. To our disappointment, we found out that with an easement, there were restrictions, like no fences, sheds, walls, trails, or buildings allowed to be constructed. Also, there were limitations on planting trees and other forms of landscaping. Stephen and I were both frustrated and lost our hope of extensions to our property.

During my prayer time that night, I asked the Lord for signs of what to do for our future, and I prayed for Holy Spirit's guidance. *That night, I dreamt of a young girl being flown up in the sky by hundreds of colourful balloons! Then she was dropped at a landscaped reserve near a lake, surrounded by a beautiful variety of colourful flowers. Nearby were lines of tall green trees. Wow, that was a picture perfect scene!*

Interpretation and Realisation

Without any doubt, that dream was God's message for us to move on and continue our plan: sell our property and move to another place convenient for our future retirement. So we made our first move by asking advice from some of our friends who had experience selling and buying a new property, which at that time was termed "upgrading." Most of their answers were positive, and our friends were happy and content with their decisions.

Both Stephen and I worried that it might take a long time before our property would sell, due to its location on a battle axe. The presence of the stormwater easement aggravated our anxiety, for we knew most buyers wouldn't consider purchasing this kind of property.

For some reason, I felt God's power and heard His message again, saying, "Be still, and know that I am your God" (Psalm 46:10). So the next day, with full confidence, Stephen made an appointment with a real estate broker. We visited him the following night and told him of our worry. To our surprise, he said that he had a client who was looking for a property with a big back yard, located in a secure and safe place, with enough room to park his six mini-buses for drop-off-pick-up-school kids purposes. The local council had already sent him several letters outlining his neighbours' complaints and street parking offenses.

Right there and then at his office, the broker rang up his client and informed him of our property, which he believed would suit his needs. Because of his client's urgent need to resolve his trouble with the local council, he asked for an appointment the next day to inspect the place. At this point, I'll let you guess! The broker said, "This is unbelievable! This is the first property I've ever sold within three days!"

We started to look for our own house now that our properly was sold at a "record-breaker" title! The same agent booked us two appointments per day to inspect properties for sale. I specifically mentioned to our family that when we inspect the house, we have to look for a spot for the corner unit that had housed the statue of the Immaculate Heart of Mary for thirteen years with us.

On the second day, the whole family voted for the last house we inspected, which miraculously was the only one with the perfect corner for the house of Mother Mary! We were blessed to own this statue through the love offerings we'd given to a religious store managed by the Missionary Sisters of Mary Queen of the World at Granville since arriving in Australia! Thank you, oh Lord!

In October 2001, with God's graces and blessings, we smoothly and happily settled into this newly-developed suburb. In July 2003, a lot of infrastructure projects were being developed in our location, particularly the construction of a major motorway called M7; we weren't aware of these when we moved there.

In December 2005, M7 motorway was completed. It stretched for forty kilometres and had 17 interchanges, 38 overpasses, and 146 bridges linking almost all the major suburbs around the western Sydney area. The M7 contractors, the Leighton and Abi Group, also constructed noise barriers to reduce noise for the residents nearby, and they planted 1.5 million native trees.

The local council constructed new parks with man-made lakes and beautiful landscapes, which adorned the place where we lived. At this point, we could visualise the realisation of my dream. Our house is located on a hill, with a panoramic view overlooking the *park with man-made lakes and fountains, surrounded by lines of tall trees!*

"Where are the flowers?" you may ask. Well, hubby and I planted white roses along the driveway, and at the back we planted a *variety of orchids of different colours.* Behind our back yard's fence, M7 contractors put up high fences as noise barriers and planted *lines of eucalyptus and some native tall trees!* My dream came to fruition in God's time and God's ways! Let God be praised in all the earth!

> *Let the heavens be glad and the earth rejoice; let the sea and everything that fills it resound; let the fields exults and everything in them. Then all the trees of the forest will sing for joy before the Lord who comes to judge the earth. (Psalm 96:11–12)*

6. Vision: A Silhouette of a Woman Covered with a Cape Appeared on the Switched-Off TV

June 24, 2004: date of the vision

On the first week of June's wintry morning, Stephen and I, together with our eldest daughter, Jasmine, went for my pre-admission to the hospital for a total right hip replacement, for which I'd fervently prayed the last seven months.

Two years prior, my specialist had advised me that only this surgery would remedy my struggle with walking due to my worn-out right hip cartilage. It was bearable in the beginning, but later on that year I was in extreme pain, especially with the cold weather. In November 2003, I submitted my application for the surgery, and I consented to the waiting time of eight to twelve months. I wasn't on a private health fund, so I waited patiently and surrendered everything to the Lord.

In April 2004, my family together with relatives and friends celebrated my fiftieth milestone-birthday with me with a buffet lunch at a Returned and Services League (RSL) restaurant in a nearby town. I requested monetary donations from the guests instead of gifts. The donations would fund the building of a house for a homeless single mother in the Philippines. It was a simple celebration but a remarkable and highly spirited one because of the noble cause. Before the party ended, I stood up, with the help of my cane, walked slowly to the front, and expressed my heartfelt gratitude to all the guests for their generosity and love offerings. I enthusiastically sent the donations to the Home Projects for the Poor and requested the organisation to note the donor as anonymous. I knew who the beneficiary was, as well as the location, so I could visit the site. After a year, the project was successfully accomplished! I was extremely happy to have had a meaningful fiftieth birthday celebration! Praise God for being a sponsor to a homeless single mother!

The last weekend of May, I got a call from the Health Department asking if I was ready to undergo the much-awaited operation! This was a big surprise, as it was earlier than the expected date! Of course, it was a loud "Yes," and I thanked and praised God for His belated birthday present to me!

The operation was successful! I felt all the love and prayers of my family, relatives, friends, and Couples for Christ community; most of all, I felt God's divine protection through the intercession of Mother Mary, with all the angels and saints.

Mid-afternoon on my third day in the hospital, my eldest daughter, Jasmine, and a couple of friends were in the room. The nurse came and requested all the visitors to leave for about ten to fifteen minutes as they changed the dressing on my wound. As I held on to the lifter's handles to support and lift up my body, *I glanced at the switched-off TV hanging on the wall. I saw a silhouette of a woman covered with a cape!* I looked up again and again and again, and she was still there! The nurse noticed my facial reactions and asked if there was something wrong. I was hesitant to tell her, because she might think I was delirious, so I just said that I was okay and it was nothing to worry about.

When she left, Jasmine and the visitors were allowed to come in. I first requested Jasmine to come in so I could show her this vision. "Yes," she answered, "I can see a silhouette of a woman there on the switched-off TV." She looked around the room, thinking there might be some reflection causing the silhouette, but she couldn't find anything.

I asked her, "Do you believe, as I do, that the woman's silhouette is Mother Mary?"

Jasmine answered with tears in her eyes. "Yes, I do." With that, she hugged me and we prayed the Rosary together with the other two friends.

Interpretation and Realisation

My specialist-surgeon told me that I would be in the hospital for approximately nine to ten days, depending on my progress. The next step was rehabilitation for two to three months in a nearby nursing home. God gave me another big surprise! Our very own one-level house was approved as my rehabilitation home because there were no steps and I had easy access to the bathroom. The height of my bed met the requirements too. It was a huge relief for my family and convenient for me!

I considered my nine days in the hospital as the best days of my life! You may ask why. First of all, I knew that I wasn't alone in the room, for I was being watched over by God and Mother Mary! It was an indescribable feeling of honour, privilege, and utmost security, as if their arms were wrapped around me, like a newly born baby. It was filled with heartfelt love and absolute care!

An emergency situation had transpired after my operation, which led me to a solo-patient room. The doctor and nurses were alarmed when I woke up from my operation! I had almost fainted when the nurse asked me to stand up, due to sudden drop of my blood pressure coupled with low potassium. The doctor said that I might need to undergo a blood transfusion if in three hours my potassium remained low. As soon as the doctor said that, Stephen went out to buy bananas. Upon his return, he told me to eat two ripe bananas straight away. His magical advice meant I avoided the scary thought of a blood transfusion! I was assigned to a one-patient room in front of the nurses' station for monitoring purposes and stayed there until I was released from the hospital after nine wonderful days. I truly felt God's love and protection, as well as Mother Mary's loving intercession for my safety.

Secondly, I felt that I was in a hotel room on a holiday, with my own ensuite bathroom and the daily visits of a housekeeper, nurse, physiotherapist, and occupational therapist. During the physiotherapy sessions, I was with Susan, a sixty-eight-year old patient whose room was next to mine. She had another patient staying with her. She popped into my room, just curious about what a solo-patient room looked like. She was impressed with what she saw and said how lucky I was to be on a private health fund. Instinctively, I felt I'd face some negative repercussions if I told her that I was also on the public health system, like her. I'd sensed her aggressive and fussy personality, so I just left it to avoid complications. It worried me that she might complain about not getting the same privilege. Honestly, I was more than on a private health fund. I was on HPHF—Heaven's Private Health Fund!

Thirdly, being a solo-patient meant there was complete silence and serenity, which gave me the opportunity to read more religious books about our faith and the lives of saints, aside from my regular prayers and daily gospel readings and mass attendance availed through the television.

Fourthly, the room was in the perfect morning sun location! I had the chance of a lifetime to watch the gorgeous morning star Venus, which sets down at the same time that the glorious morning sun rises up over the horizon! Oh, what a magnificent scenery! I was in total awe!

My vision of the appearance of the woman's silhouette covered with a cape on that switched-off TV was a manifestation of God's love and faithfulness to His promises and of Mother Mary's love and protection over me! Amen!

> *"But let those who take refuge in you rejoice; let them ever sing for joy. Let your deliverance shield them, that those who love Your name may praise You in gladness" (Psalm 5:11).*

7. Vision: A Man's Face Turned Old and Then White

December 28, 2004: date of the vision

We'd been living in the neighbourhood for three years and had established quite a few friendships. I felt a special bond with a particular couple, Nick and Medi, who were in their retirement years. I especially liked the old man because I associated him with my Tatay due to his age, build, and looks. Nick was also a very friendly and helpful neighbour, who was always ready to give a hand. When Stephen went home to the Philippines to visit his sick father, I got regular calls from Nick just checking how I was if I needed anything. I felt so secure, even though I was alone without Stephen. Very often, Medi called out over the fence just to hand me her delicious specialty dishes, which always tasted to perfection. I was truly blessed to have good neighbours like Nick and Medi!

During the Christmas holidays of 2004, Nick and Medi invited us to a party at their friends' home, who lived within the neighbourhood. We were familiar with them as well. After lunch, the host called the guests to gather at the back, and I expected some sort of games or gift exchange. There were tables set, ready for playing cards. To my surprise, almost everyone comfortably found their seats and eagerly wanted to play! Stephen and I felt like fish out of water, because we had no idea how to play any kind of card games.

Just at that moment, we were saved by the bell! Nick called us to sit with him at the back, which was away from the noisy card players. Medi was also among the card players. Stephen and I happily chatted with Nick for hours and enjoyed each other's company. We talked about work, family, and life's challenges. *Then I saw something strange about Nick's face! While he was talking to us, his face seemed to be growing older and older and older; then it turned white!* I quickly removed my focus from him and instead looked up to the sky and closed my eyes while praying for him. Instinctively, I felt that Nick had some major health issues. I wanted to ask him about his health, but he was engrossed in some funny storytelling with my husband about his workplace. He seemed to be happy, and I didn't want to spoil the joyful moments of their conversation.

Before the party ended, I prayed hard for a chance to speak to Medi, just to ask about her husband's health and not to mention anything about what I envisioned. When I saw Medi stand up to go to the restroom, I grabbed the moment. She told me that her husband was in perfect health and she wasn't aware of anything unusual about his health. In fact, she said that tomorrow they were driving to Canberra with their visitors from overseas. I wished them a safe and enjoyable journey, but inside I felt worried, so I fervently prayed for Nick. Dear Lord, please look after him, and I pray that what I saw on him today was nothing.

Interpretation and Realisation

The vision I saw on Nick's face that day was a vision of a very sick man physically. He was the kindest and friendliest older man I'd ever met, not only in our new neighbourhood but in all of Australia, our second home. Instantly, I had a soft spot for him, as if he were my father.

In January 2005, I visited my daughter-in-law in the hospital, who had just given birth to their first child and our third grandchild. I was about to leave the premises when Medi, looking haggard and worried, walked in the door of the hospital. She saw me and came rushing toward me with tears in her eyes, saying, "My husband was diagnosed with leukemia." I hugged her tight, because the vision I saw was not good. I instinctively went with her inside to visit Nick, but he was asleep. I didn't look at him anymore, because I was scared to see that face again, so I just prayed for healing and a miracle from the Lord.

I told Stephen about my vision and asked him to ask Nick if he still had some missions and concerns unaccomplished in his life. The answer was a firm "Yes."

"I want my only daughter to get married in church before I cross the bar," he said. Their only daughter lived with them, together with her partner, without the blessing of the sacrament of matrimony. It's every parent's dream to see their children settled and married in church. This was Nick's absolute dream!

Without wasting a single moment, Stephen immediately contacted Father Paulo, our loving and compassionate parish priest, and confided in him this request from a dying man. He exerted all his efforts to expedite the date of the wedding, as every day Nick's health was deteriorating. After two months, he was successfully given the approval for the earliest wedding date. Praise God!

When the wedding march began playing, all were in tears when they saw the father of the bride in a wheelchair join in the procession. It was a solemn, blessed, and heartbreaking scene! At that moment, I wasn't scared to look at him, and I saw a sweet, happy, and radiant face of the father of the bride, with sparkles of peace, contentment, and happiness in his eyes!

Not too long after that, Nick, whom I deeply respected, passed away. I'm very sure that he is now in Heaven with the angels and saints, his eternal home, which the heavenly Father prepared for him.

> *"Write this: Happy from now are the dead who die in the Lord. 'Yes,' says the Spirit, 'let them rest from their labours, since their good works go with them'" (Revelation 14:13).*

8. Dream: Kuya Nico's Face so Close to Mine, Asking for Help

July 13, 2011: date of the dream

Time flew by, and we'd been in Australia for twenty-three years. Our three children were all married and had their own homes, so Stephen and I lived by ourselves in an empty nest. We were so thankful for God's graces and blessings, and we now had the opportunity to travel. On the top of our bucket list was to join pilgrimage tours in the Holy Land, Marian Tours, and

Steps of Saint Paul in the chronological order of the Christian faith's history. The last listed pilgrimage tour was the Graces of Eastern Europe, highlighting the apparition of the Blessed Virgin Mary in Medjugorje, Bosnia. We believed that in this way we would travel with Jesus, as well as Mother Mary, and discover the holy and sacred places they travelled to in the past.

But one day I received a mobile message from my sister-in-law in the Philippines, saying that Kuya Nico, my elder brother, had a brain aneurysm and was in intensive care in the hospital. It was life and death, so Stephen and I, without any hesitation, booked our flights home. Sadly and unexpectedly, our travel plan and top priority now was to visit my sick brother.

The earliest flight we could get had a stop-over in Singapore and another three-hour wait for the next flight to Manila. During the stop-over, I surrendered everything to God and spoke to Kuya Nico in my prayers, telling him that if he was in pain, he had to go and not to wait for me. I promised to take care of the finances. After fifteen minutes, I received a mobile message that sadly Kuya Nico had already passed away. With deep sadness and sorrow, we continued our flight to Manila and prayed for the repose of his soul to rest in peace.

Everything was all arranged for the mass and funeral of Kuya Nico. We met our whole clan and felt a mixture of sadness and joy at seeing each other. Kuya Nico was survived by his wife and three children. The youngest, Kathy, age thirteen, had just finished her elementary education, which meant she would be in high school at the end of July. It was heartbreaking to say goodbye again to our loved ones and relatives, with the uncertainty of when we would see them again.

Two days after the funeral, we left for Australia with the aim of transferring money to my sister-in-law's bank account as soon as we arrived home, to support Kathy's enrolment fees. We'd spent our allocated money for the trip, like paying the hospital bills, funeral costs, and other miscellaneous expenses. Because of this, I wasn't able to leave cash for Kathy. My generous husband happily agreed to my plan of supporting her studies until college, since our children were all married and financially stable.

That very first night back in Australia, I dreamed of my deceased brother so clearly and distinctly. I just saw his face close to my face, asking for help for the education of his youngest daughter, Kathy. And I answered, "Yes, don't worry, I will." It was quick and then gone.

In the morning, I received a call from my sister-in-law asking for support for her daughter's enrolment.

Interpretation and Realisation

Kuya Nico and I had a very unique relationship. He was only one year older than me. At seven, he was enrolled in year 1 of his elementary education at the Catholic school run by the Religious of the Virgin Mary. I remember that when he went to school, I would cry the whole day because I wanted to go too. On the third day, Aunt Nina took me to school and asked a big favour from the nuns—to allow me to be with my brother in year 1, even unofficially due to my young age. The school counsellor agreed, as long as I behaved and was a good girl. After three months, the school officially enrolled me because I had shown good academic achievement, even better than my brother. The school year ended so fast, and I certainly remembered my name being called onto the stage to get medals of honour.

Life is a roller coaster of emotions. After the joy of passing that year with flying colours came the very sad news that our mother had passed away in the hospital due to internal haemorrhage. This was the time that we as siblings became close, but I noticed that in the succeeding days, months, and years, I was looked up to by my brothers as if I were the eldest. Everyone thought that my elder brother and I were twins, because we started and finished both elementary and secondary school at the same time. I had been supportive of my two brothers when they asked favours for their own families' needs, because I felt so much more blessed than them in every aspect in life.

Since our family had migrated to Australia in 1988, Kuya Nico wasn't able to get a stable job to sufficiently provide for his family's needs and support his children's education. He was sickly and suffered from high blood pressure due to the hot and humid climate of the Philippines. Also, genetically, hypertension and heart and stroke issues were a common cause of death in our family. His alcohol addiction never totally left him because of his depression due to his health and financial problems. His submission to alcohol became his comfort and security. So every now and then, I sent some financial support for his family just to help them with their daily needs. At thirty-eight years of age, Kuya Nico had his first stroke. At age forty-six, he had his second stroke. The third time, sadly, he didn't survive. He died at only fifty-eight years of age.

Even beyond life on earth, I said my yes to the favour my deceased brother asked of me in the dream. I faithfully kept my promise to Kuya Nico by sending Kathy's school fees every year without fail for the last ten years up to the date I'm writing this book. Kathy will be graduating with a Bachelor of Science in Business Management next year, in April 2022. She has shown exemplary academic performance, even being on the Dean's List. I feel so privileged to help and support her, which is the key to her and her family's brighter future. No one would be prouder and happier than her Papa in heaven!

God's unconditional love and compassion to me had designed me to be like Him. I praise and thank God for being an instrument in accomplishing Kuya Nico's desire for his daughter's education and fulfilling my promise to provide the help he asked of me through a dream! Let God be praised forever!

> *Bless the Lord, my soul; all my inmost being, bless His holy name! Bless the Lord, my soul, and do not forget all His kindness. He forgives all my*

> *sins, and heals all my sickness; He redeems my life from destruction, and crowns me with love and compassion; He gives fulfillment to my years, and renews my youth like the eagle's. (Psalm 103:1–5)*

9. Dream: Blessed Mother Mary Seated with a Golden Crown on Her Head

August 15, 2013: date of the dream

The Feast of the Assumption of the Virgin Mary is celebrated as a holy day of obligation by Catholics, and it's also as a public holiday in some Catholic countries, like the Philippines, Spain, and Malta to mention a few. A holy day of obligation in the Catholic Church is a religious feast day on which Catholics must attend mass and spend the day abstaining from hard and unimportant work.

That night, we attended the mass of the Feast of the Assumption, and I was deeply inspired to travel to and visit the traces of the Virgin Mary's apparitions in different parts of the world, like Our Lady of Lourdes in France, Our Lady of Fatima in Portugal, and the Black Madonna in Monserrat, Spain. As a couple nearly reaching retirement age, we were seriously looking for a pilgrimage tour to these places.

That night, I dreamed that we were in a car with a couple of friends, travelling a long, winding road going downhill and uphill, looking for a particular church. We felt like we were lost, so we stopped and asked a local. He politely said, "Follow this road, then turn left three times, and you will see the church." Finally, we saw the church at a distance! As we got closer, we saw what looked like a huge gazebo, a circular building with big, bold words written around the sides: "MAGNIFICAT, MAGNIFICAT, MAGNIFICAT, MAGNIFICAT." In the middle was the Virgin Mary seated with a golden crown on her head! Then we went inside the church and saw all the people dressed in white, with blue name tags hanging around their necks. It was a very solemn and sacred place, and we heard the angelic voices of the choir singing the beautiful Marian songs after each decade of the Rosary. I felt like it was Heaven!

Interpretation and Realisation

After our Holy Land Pilgrimage Tour in October 2011, the next item on our bucket list was to join the Marian Pilgrimage Tour. Stephen and I agreed that this was our main goal for the next year, 2014. We offered masses and lots of prayers for the intention of finding the right tour. I couldn't wait for this tour to take place and to visit the holy places where Mother Mary appeared, all in one main message of repentance: "Penance! Penance! Penance! Pray to God for sinners!" Then one day God answered our prayers! Our leaders from the Couples for Christ Australia community had organized a Marian Pilgrimage Tour, and they eagerly invited us. We happily signed and submitted all necessary papers and deposited partial payment for our travel fares for the next year.

Our Marian Tour Group of sixteen people, including the spiritual director, left Sydney in September 2014.You can just imagine my eagerness to see how my dream would unfold now that our travel goal had come to fruition!

Our tour guide told us that the walk from our hotel in France to the Shrine of Our Lady of Lourdes would be about 1.5 kilometres in length. We were all set and ready in our comfortable walking shoes and backpacks, and off we went, following our tour guide towards the shrine. There were thousands of pilgrims of different ages, races, and nationalities from all parts of the world. The Shrine of Our Lady of Lourdes receives approximately six million pilgrims and visitors every year, all with one goal of paying homage and praying to the Virgin Mary, Mother of Jesus, our Saviour!

The tour guide signalled everybody for a left turn after around two hundred meters, and then we walked all straight ahead. After another three hundred meters, he signalled for another left turn and then continued walking, with quick stops to regain energy. The guide said that after around four hundred meters, we'd take a last left turn and then walk straight ahead to the huge white entry gate to the Shrine of Our Lady of Lourdes. *I counted all the left turns we took and, to my surprise, there were three in total, just like what I saw in my dream!*

As we were at the entry, I was in ecstasy when I saw a *huge golden crown on the Virgin Mary* as part of the Shrine. Anyone who has visited this shrine understands what I mean here. It's a stunning heavenly beauty that can't be missed! This scene now in front of me had been a part of my dream. I thought that maybe at the next site there would be the scene of the Blessed Mother Mary seated with the golden crown on her head.

At the Shrine of Our Lady of Lourdes, I saw hundreds of elderly people in wheelchairs being pushed by men and women dressed in white, with "Volunteer" written on name tags along with their name. These volunteers helped and cared for the sick and pushed the old people in wheelchairs toward the miraculous water in the spring for a bath or just to drink it with the hope of healing and regaining strength.

Stephen and I were blessed to meet Mila, a Filipina volunteer from Germany. According to her, every year volunteers from different countries visit for one to two weeks and carry out this noble mission of helping and caring for the sick and elderly. When she visited this holy shrine, she was inspired and vowed to be one of them, so she inquired at the office at the site and was told the whole process. Mila told us that she had been a volunteer for three years now.

In my dream, *the people inside the church, all dressed in white with blue name tags hanging around their necks*, represented the actual volunteers in Lourdes! I was in awe just looking at the scene right in front of me, because it was almost the same scene as I saw in my dream!

Oh my God! Thank you, Jesus, for the fruition of our goal and deepest desire, for the privilege to see this Shrine of Our Lady of Lourdes and for revealing the meaning of my dream that night of the Feast of the Assumption of your Beloved Mother, and my mother too!

Another surprise unfolded on this tour when we visited Our Lady of Monserrat in Catalonia, Spain. The Shrine is located on the serrated mountain ranges and receives around three million pilgrims every year. The statue has always been considered one of the most celebrated images in Spain for its unique colour, thus it's also known as the Black Madonna, Patroness of Catalonia. The statue was originally a lighter tone but eventually turned darker, either due to prolonged exposure to smoke or caused by a varnish used as a paint sealant. The statue was repainted black by successive generations of restorers.

We entered the shrine and went closer to the altar, and this was what I saw in front of me: *The statue of Our Lady of Monserrat was seated behind a protective sheet of glass, wearing a golden crown on her head!* This symbolises the Blessed Virgin Mary's virtues of humility, purity, and obedience, which equates with power, glory, and the sovereignty of a Queen, as Queen of Heaven and Earth! Slowly but surely the details of my dream had transpired right in front of my eyes, with perfect contentment and overflowing happiness! Thank you, O Lord, my God!

> *"Enter His gates with thanksgiving and His courts with praise; give thanks to Him and bless His name. For the Lord is good and His love lasts forever and faithfulness through all generations." (Psalm 100:4-5)*

10. Dream: A Distressed Woman inside the Grilled Window and Locked House, Waving Her Hand at Me

November 2, 2015: date of the dream

In the Christian Church, November is the Feast and Solemnity of All Saints, both known and unknown, who have attained Heaven. The next day is the remembrance of all our departed loved ones and is known as All Souls Day. These two days make me contemplate that life on earth is only temporary and we are transient pilgrims here, which is a constant reminder of the importance of living a spirit-filled, fulfilled, and productive life. That's why aside from remembering and praying for the souls of our departed loved ones, I also regard the month of November as a remembrance-day of our own souls still living here on earth.

That night I dreamed of a small village, with lines of small houses uniformly built of plain hollow blocks and corrugated iron. The frontage had two grilled tiny windows, like on prison cells, and a wooden entry door. As I strolled along the narrow and rough road, I saw a distressed woman waving her hand at me, holding a key, and signalling me to open the door. I instantly thought that she was locked inside the house. Without hesitation, I succumbed to her urgent plea, rushed to her, got the key, and opened the door. She hugged me so tight with cries of relief and gratitude!

I woke up with tears in my eyes due to the extreme emotions of relief and joy of the woman's freedom! Who was this woman? Why was she locked inside her house?

Interpretation and Realisation

According to Mission Australia, domestic and family violence is disturbingly common in our country, and it results in homelessness among both women and men. National statistics state that one in six women and one in sixteen men have experienced violence by an intimate partner. These figures help us understand the gravity of the situation, but alarmingly, many victims of domestic and family violence will never report their experience. With many incidents going unreported, the violence may be much worse than we think.

Knowing of the presence of this society's disease, it's possible that just around the corner or even next door to us lives a woman, child, or even a man who is a victim of violence and abuse beyond our imagination. This is sometimes a cruel world because of people in darkness.

When I woke up from that dream, I felt that the distressed woman could be suffering from violence and abuse from someone and pleading for help. I believe that a woman has a role to play to make a difference in this world by emulating the virtues of Mother Mary, which are humility, obedience, patience, charity, continual prayer, and strong faith.

I belong to the ministry known as Handmaids of the Lord, which operates under the umbrella of Couples for Christ. Its evangelistic mission is to bring women closer to God. I knew that God wanted me to help this disturbed woman, but who was she? In my daily prayers, I listed the intention of discovering this woman as my top priority, because I felt the urgency to act on this as opportunity allowed me. It was a matter of life and death.

By the end of November, I was assigned to give an inspirational talk to the group of women I served in the northern region, as the last activity for the year. I spoke about Feminine Genius, a topic popularised by St John Paul II as an honour to the Blessed Virgin Mary and a tribute to all women. Mainly, I touched on the importance of women to society, saying that "the hands that rock the cradle are the hands that rule the world." Even behind the scenes, women can play significant roles in society, which is why they're often called quiet or silent achievers.

During the fellowship, I noticed a restless woman sitting in a corner alone. She seemed ready to go home but then turned back towards the kitchen and got a drink. Instinctively, I grabbed that moment to get a drink as well, just to say hello. She smiled at me, though I noticed her sad eyes. She bravely applauded the talk I'd delivered and said that she was deeply touched. She could hardly control the flow of tears. I hugged her and said, "It's perfectly okay to cry!" Now I could really hear her sobbing on my chest. While praying for her, I requested that we stay in the quieter room next to the kitchen.

Together we prayed to the Holy Spirit for healing, which later prompted her to unload her heavy burden. Mel (her name) cried in anguish and pain and said, "I am nothing. I can't even be a proper mother to my own child!" She fearfully confessed that her partner, Fabian, bashed and abused her and just used her to earn money. Mel was the breadwinner, while he enjoyed his life as a king with his world of wine, women, and cards. He paid a part-time baby sitter so that Mel can be a full-time worker. I was dumbfounded while I listened to her appalling story! I thought I was watching a shocking and dramatic movie! But this was for real! I couldn't believe that there were evil men like Fabian in the world. *This has to end!*

Mel was *the distressed woman in my dream, who was in a grilled window like in a prison cell!* In reality, she'd been imprisoned by this satanic man for three years who urgently needed to be stopped. The next day, I secretly gave Mel the names and phone numbers of agencies to call and discretely report this domestic violence. She was hesitant because of the fear that Fabian might kill her and their child. With the power of prayer, finally Mel was convinced to do this bravely, and I assured her that she'd be supported by the welfare agency.

I dreamed of a small village, with lines of small houses uniformly built and made of plain hollow blocks and corrugated iron. The frontage had two grilled tiny windows, like on a prison cell. This symbolised the existence of many more "Mels" in the world who are victims of abuse, fear, and a complete loss of dignity as women. These victims and prisoners must be freed and the evil ones be imprisoned and crushed into pieces like the serpent's head.

At this present time of 2021, Mel and her five-year-old daughter, Marie, are happily settled in the western region and have started a new life in the Holy Spirit. She's not heard from Fabian since he was locked up in jail for involvements in gang crimes. He's behind a tiny, iron grilled window! Indeed, God is a *just God*! Amen!

> *"A faithful God without injustice, how righteous and upright is he" (Deuteronomy 32:4).*

> *"Justice and virtue are the foundation of your throne; love and faithfulness go before you" (Psalm 89:14).*

11. Dream: A Spacious Arena Filled with People Singing and Praising God

February 10, 2016: date of the dream

Last night I dreamed of a spacious arena filled with people singing and praising God with all their might! A very powerful voice reverberated through the huge arena, coming from a passionate speaker. It was followed by the fellowship of brothers and sisters from a group happily chatting while enjoying the different kinds of food being sold in food stalls. I saw a multitude of people of different nationalities gathered together, but in groups identified through a placard or banner revealing what country they came from! What a vibrant and colourful picture!

Then I woke up in awe! I was so happy to see such a scenario of people gathered with one faith.

Interpretation and Realisation

Saint Paul, formerly Saul, was a former persecutor of Jesus. In fact, he was present himself when Saint Stephen, the first martyred apostle, was stoned to death for proclaiming to the Jewish people that Jesus is the Messiah, Saviour, and Redeemer. When Saul was converted and God named him Paul, he became the most persecuted apostle and is regarded as one of the most important figures of the Apostolic Age!

With feelings of excitement and eagerness, I looked forward to our next pilgrimage tour, The Footsteps of Saint Paul, which was scheduled in the next two months. This was precisely the reason why I dreamed of such scenario—an amazing beauty of love and passion toward one's faith and conviction! This clearly explained my utmost enthusiasm in joining this tour, which would surely deepen my faith as well as Stephen's.

The pilgrimage tour would lead us to Saint Paul's ministry of evangelisation, spreading the good news in different parts of Greece, Turkey, and Malta. He travelled over ten thousand miles proclaiming the gospel of Jesus Christ during his three journeys. This much-anticipated tour would walk us through his third and longest journey, over land through present day Turkey and then across the Aegean Sea to Greece. This was the pastoral journey in which he revisited the churches he had founded to strengthen and give them his further instruction.

Finally, in April 2016, our group left Australia and landed safely in Greece. The very next day, we eagerly started with prayers led by our spiritual director, Father Alan, and then headed to Philippi. In awe, I knelt in front of Lydia's Baptistry Chapel in honour of Lydia, the first woman baptised and evangelised by Saint Paul, who offered her dwelling as an assembly place for meetings of the faithful.

Here in Philippi, I got stunned into silence and felt goosebumps when we walked on the well-paved roads, formerly rugged-rocky-dusty roads, which left traces of Saint Paul's steps, together with his followers. I can't believe that I literally stepped on the path he took in approximately 49–51 AD! I felt so overwhelmed and consider this the apex or culmination of the tour!

Then the tour guide led us to the site where Paul and Silas were arrested, flogged, and imprisoned for being a public nuisance. While in prison, they sat with their feet in stocks, singing hymns, until at midnight an earthquake broke open the prison doors, setting the prisoners free. The jailer feared that his superiors would blame him for the jail break, so he prepared to run himself through with a sword rather than face the punishment. Paul and Silas convinced him not to harm himself; they preached the gospel to him, and he was saved, along with his entire household that night! What an exceptional story of conviction on one's faith!

Then we headed to Thessalonica, where Paul preached in the synagogues. Many Jews and Greeks were convinced of the truth and were baptised. At the synagogue we visited, *there were hundreds and hundreds of pilgrims singing songs and praising God* (same as what I saw in my dream). We joined them and followed what they were doing. Then at the ceremony, the priest blessed Saint Paul's icon, stating "The Preacher-Evangeliser for Christ." All the pilgrims, including us, clapped our hands, like a standing ovation, and ended the liturgy with the sign of the cross. Outside the synagogue, *some people were selling all types of snacks for the pilgrims and at the same time greeting each other as brothers and sisters in the same faith* (as in my dream).

Wow! I was in tears because I remembered that dream of a *spacious arena, filled with people singing and praising God.* And now it was right here in front of me! The arena symbolises a place for public events, where sports, entertainment, or even a battle are held. In this case, Saint Paul's evangelisation was regarded as a battle during those times; he was arrested, flogged, and imprisoned.

A powerful voice reverberated in the huge arena, coming from a passionate speaker. This was none other than Saint Paul himself. He was fearless, bold, and daring, for he believed that God had called him; therefore, He would be with him. In fact, while in Ephesus, Paul heard a prophecy that should he return to Jerusalem, he would be imprisoned. The churches he founded pleaded for him not to go. But Paul felt the call from Christ to continue to meet whatever God willed for him. With strong conviction he said, "Do not be conformed to the world where you live, but rather be transformed through the renewal of your mind. You must discern the will of God—what is pleasing, and what is perfect" (Romans 12:2).

Thank you, oh Lord God, for being able to join this beautiful, touching, and inspiring pilgrimage of The Footsteps of Saint Paul, which deepened our faith towards Your heavenly kingdom! Amen!

> *"Make the Lord your delight, and He will grant your heart's desire. Commit your way to the Lord; put your trust in Him and let Him act" (Psalm 37:4–5).*

12. Dream: A Woman Yelled at Her Husband and Disturbed the Quiet Night

March 18, 2016: date of the dream

Time flies so fast! We've been living in this neighbourhood for fifteen years now and truly find it so peaceful, safe, and secure in a cul-de-sac. Our neighbours are friendly, and we usually greet each other with "Good morning" and "How are you?" Or we simply wave our hands every day when leaving for work in the morning or arriving home at night. The majority of the residents are young couples, some with young children and some without.

One morning, I woke up troubled by this dream. *A woman yelled at her husband and disturbed the quiet night. Then the dogs continuously barked madly! What's happening? I was curious, so I peeked out of the window and saw a man smoking outside the house while inside, a woman was still loudly talking and then mumbling and sobbing. Then slowly it became quiet, until the sound of crickets could be heard again.* What was that dream about?

I prayed my usual morning offerings and grace and headed off to work. It was terribly busy at work, and the day went by quickly. On my way home, I tried to figure out the meaning of the dream, but nothing came to me. Confidently, I said that slowly but surely something would come up through the enlightenment of the Holy Spirit. I included in my daily prayers the couple I had seen in my dream, for I felt that somewhere, somehow, a couple was in the midst of turmoil and on the brink of separation.

Interpretation and Realisation

Before Stephen and I got married, we attended a required series of talks on the sacrament of marriage before facing God and the church for the sacred mass and liturgy of matrimony. The main point I took away from that teaching was that there should be three persons involved in marriage, not only two. Why three? The priest explained, "The man, the woman, and most importantly God in the midst of them. In order to practically fulfill the famous marriage vow 'Till death do us part,' the couple must put God in the middle of their relationship. They pray and attend mass together and actively serve in the church activities. Spiritual life is the major ingredient in a successful marriage." I am a witness of the truth behind this!

Next month, in April, Stephen and I will celebrate our fortieth wedding anniversary. All praises to you, oh God Almighty! As Australia is a first world country, divorce and separation is more common than in third world countries. This statement is based on the theory of my late professor in theology during my college years. I clearly remember his words: "When a country's economy is low, its morality is high; when the country's economy is high, its morality is low." He continued his lecture with examples of broken marriages in first world and third world countries. The Philippines is still considered a third world country, and being a Catholic country, divorce is illegal. That's why in cases of marital problems, the Catholic Church extends support through counselling and other support programs in order to resolve issues. While in first world countries, like Australia, this issue may not be regarded as much of a priority due to the busyness of people. It's more convenient to separate or divorce. So sad to know that in such situations, the children suffer such pain and trauma. If only couples followed the three-persons-in-a-marriage formula, this would be avoided.

Three weeks later, Ruby, my close friend who lives in the western region area, called me. I immediately noticed her sad voice. As soon as I asked if she was all right, she started sobbing and could hardly talk. I told her to cry and pour out the heaviness of her heart. When she had settled down, she told me the depressing news that her husband, George, had left her and their two children for a younger woman. They'd only been married for eight years. George was a workaholic and rarely home on weekends to spend quality time with his family. Ruby wanted the whole family to attend Sunday mass together, but George was never there. Then this shocking news was revealed, which Ruby never in her wildest dream expected to hear. She'd trusted that George was just hardworking, even on Saturdays and Sundays, which she regarded as a sacrifice for their family's needs. The sky fell on her head when she found out that George was with a younger woman in the city! She was completely devastated and asked herself, "Where did I go wrong?"

I felt so sorry that her marriage had suddenly crashed into pieces, like a castle in the sand completely swept away by the waves of the ocean! The marriage failed because the third person in the marriage wasn't God but another woman!

As Ruby cried out her anguish and pain, I prayed for her. With much pity, I offered for her and the two children to stay with us that weekend so we could talk properly and consider her next move. She appreciated that very much, but her loving and understanding mother-in-law had already asked them to stay with her. And that was great news! She had the support of George's mother, who hated what her son had done, as it opened the painful wound of her own history of her husband's infidelity!

Her own son's betrayal of his marriage vows with Ruby was an exact reflection of her own emotional pain and grief after her husband's adultery, who left her and young George for a younger woman. There had been no trace of him since, as I gathered from Ruby's disclosure of her mother-in-law's sad story.

As of this date in 2021, Ruby occasionally calls to give me updates on her journey as a single mother. She still lives with her mother-in-law, who requested her and the children to stay with her until she dies. Much to her surprise, the mother-in-law even wrote her name in the will as the sole beneficiary of her house! A marriage between a husband and wife may fail and end, but in some cases, an in-law's relationship lasts forever! This rare life journey reminded me of the Bible story of Ruth and her example of faithfulness in her choice to stay with Naomi, her mother-in-law, until the end of her days. I was so happy for Ruby and proud of her faith and strength of character!

In my dream, *the woman yelling at the husband* was Ruby. She was mad at him due to his infidelity. George was *the man outside smoking*, which symbolises his relaxed state, because he had made his firm decision to leave his family. The dream showed that after that commotion, peace and quietness of the night was regained, as both sides had moved on in their own lives—George with the younger woman pursuing an enticing life in the city, and Ruby with God's grace finding the genuine love and support of her mother-in-law, who adores her two grandchildren. Out of sincere gratitude, Ruby remained faithful to her. She moved on in her life's odyssey as a single mother and, together with her mother-in-law, lived a simple, contented, happy, and peaceful life!

> *"The master answered: 'Well done, good and faithful servant, since you have been faithful in little things, I will entrust much more to you. Come and share the joy of your master'" (Matthew 25:21).*

13. Dream: A Man's Heart Is Like a Corroded Iron!

June 3, 2016: date of the dream

That wintry night, I tossed and turned as I prayed the Rosary and then fell into a deep sleep and dreamed. *The setting was at the hospital, as there were some nurses around the bed where a man was lying with an open chest! I could only see the chest, so I didn't know who the man was. But what struck me most was that I could see the man's heart, and it looked like a corroded iron!*

I woke up with a heavy sigh and wondered who the man in my dream was. I said my morning prayers and started my normal daily routine, offering the whole day of prayers and fasting, with the sincere hope that the Holy Spirit would guide and show me, or even just give me a clue about the dream.

Two days passed, and my prayers and fasting were still on because I hadn't received any clue or signs yet, but I was still hopeful that I would get one very soon. In the morning, I received an overseas call from Liam, my youngest brother, who lived in Chicago, Illinois. I was extremely happy to hear from him. He was my only brother now, as Kuya Nico, our elder brother, had already passed away five years earlier.

Both Liam and I were extremely happy to exchange news about our respective families, especially our children. Liam was a smart and vibrant spokesman, so finding jobs was no problem for him. He wasn't even a high school graduate, yet he managed to go to America! Since we'd left our beloved country, I'd surrendered Liam to God's divine providence, so I knew God followed and guided him all the way. I also asked the intercession of our Blessed Mother to keep him away from evil and lead him always to the right path.

He had stayed in USA for almost ten years now as a self-employed home renovator. Liam shared his struggles in starting his life overseas, which is a common experience of all migrants. He persevered and battled over all the trials and challenges he encountered because he was focused on the better future of his three children. Finally, after ten years, he had reached his goal to sponsor his wife and children from the Philippines to live with him in the land of milk and honey. Documents and other legal requirements were all submitted for processing. I cheerfully told him, "What a remarkable accomplishment, my dearest brother, and I am the proudest sister ever! In Heaven, Tatay, Nanay, and Kuya Nico are extremely proud of you!" At the end of the phone line, I heard his sniffles and felt his joy, but with anxiety.

That's great news! I was so ecstatic, especially looking back at Liam's complete transformation from drugs to dignified life! Oh Lord God, thank you for keeping my brother safe under your wings. But my overwhelming happiness didn't last long, as he mentioned about his health issues. His heart specialist said that he had to undergo a heart valve transplant immediately! Without a second thought, Stephen booked our flights to Chicago once we learned the exact date of his delicate operation. I just felt that it was the right thing to do as his elder sister—to be with him at this time of his fragile life.

We arrived safely, and I saw the sparkles and tears from Liam's eyes as mixed emotions were expressed from both of us as "long-time orphans!" After a long evening of catching up, we retired for the night after we prayed the Rosary, in which he happily joined and participated, ready for the next day's battle.

I stayed in the hospital's chapel, fervently praying for Liam's successful operation and completely surrendering him to the Lord. Then the surgeon called and gave us the great news that everything went well! He said, "Your brother incredibly surpassed this very delicate heart valve transplant! But what amazed me most was the miraculous survival of your brother for fifty-six years, because his old heart valve was like a 'corroded iron' that should only belong to an eighty-year-old man, not one his age! It was indeed the right timing for the valve to be replaced."

Interpretation and Realisation

"His heart valve was like a corroded iron" were the exact words of the surgeon and the same vision I saw in my dream! The man was my youngest brother, Liam! Because we were orphaned early and deprived of maternal care, no one in the family knew that Liam had been born with very tiny tubes in his aortic heart valves, which caused extreme damage of his valve. Providentially, he had lived a very active lifestyle. He'd participated in a basketball tournament and other athletic games, which helped a lot with his breathing struggles and in living fifty-six years, which was a huge bonus, according to the surgeon.

Liam and I had a very deep and strong bond, more of a mother to a son relationship instead of an elder sister to a younger brother. He was only one year old when our Nanay died. Thus, our relationship was one of a kind! But sadly, he grew up spoilt by Tatay, who seemed to be compensating for the untimely loss of a mother by giving in to all of his whims and wants. Liam eventually joined the wrong crowd, in spite of my good advice and reminders, which just fell on deaf ears. I didn't give up hope but prayed fervently that one day he would be touched by God's grace, and his eyes would be opened to the light of truth, goodness, and holiness. True enough, God listened to my persistent prayers, and he became a transformed man and had settled down as a family man before we migrated to Australia. My gratitude for God's goodness and faithfulness in this successful operation was to the fullest and beyond words. Oh, thank you, Lord God Almighty!

Liam was released from the hospital after five days. He felt so victorious and looked forward to his complete recovery so he could continue his pending home renovation projects and complete the sponsorship process for his family. We spent another two days with him, looked after him, and cooked his favourite foods. We made sure that these two days were quality time, as we weren't sure when we'd see him again in person. Thank goodness for the modern technology of Skype, Messenger chats, and FaceTime as means of communications so we can still see and talk to each other, regardless of time and distance!

With heavy but peaceful heart, Stephen and I departed for Australia. After long hours of travel, we landed home safely. I went straight to bed to rest my tired body, but my soul was overwhelmingly filled with happiness and peace.

Another roller coaster of emotions then happened! The next day, we were shocked and devastated to hear the depressing and heartrending news from the landlady who took good care of Liam. He'd been rushed back to the hospital due to severe chest pain, and tragically he didn't make it but passed away while in the ambulance! Oh no! My Lord God Almighty! But why? I was so heartbroken, and I wept the whole day with the question in my mind: Why, why, Lord?

The next day during the Sunday mass, God answered my cry of anguish and questioning through the readings from Wisdom 9:13–16:

> *Indeed, who can know the intentions of God? Who can discern the plan of the Lord? For human reasoning is timid and the plans of our mind are uncertain; a perishable body is a burden for the soul and our tent of clay weighs down the active mind. We are barely able to know about the things of earth, and it is a struggle to understand what is close to us; who, then, can hope to understand heavenly things?*

As the reader proclaimed the Word of God, I cried for forgiveness for questioning God and doubting His divine will for my brother. God spoke to me loud and clear through those powerful words! Yes, who can comprehend God's will? Who am I to question God's wisdom? I felt so little, with my heart filled with guilt and shame! Oh God, forgive me, have mercy on me, a sinner!

From then on, I felt so peaceful with a sense of total acceptance of my youngest brother's death. Though he left an unfinished mission of bringing his family to America, I am proud to be a witness of his tremendous accomplishment of rebuilding our ancestral home, where he stayed with his family when we left and migrated to Australia. The old Spanish style, two-storey house was ruined during the volcanic eruption of Mount Pinatubo in 1991. Liam was able to rebuilt it into a contemporary two-storey house with a penthouse on top, which he said was reserved for us when we visited for a holiday. He was a hero in making for that long-time dream of Tatay, who inherited this ancestral home and planned to have it renovated. Liam had unbelievably executed Tatay's dream far beyond expectations! He was able to send his three children to school, and they all have stable jobs. Two of them are now married with two children each. The eldest son and his family dwell in this ancestral home together with the devoted widowed mother, who's busy babysitting the gorgeous grandchildren.

Reflecting on all of these blessings, I can't help but say these words: "Oh my brother Liam, indeed you had a short life but a huge one!" My soul was filled with joy and thanksgiving at God's absolute love and divine protection toward Liam, and I envisioned his exuberant and peaceful surroundings, with all the angels and saints in God's Heavenly Kingdom, as he reunited with Tatay, Nanay, and Kuya Nico! Oh my God, I exalt you and praise you with all my mind, with all my strength, with all my heart, and with all my soul. Amen!

> *"Stand at the crossroads and look, and ask for the paths of former times, ask where the good way lies, take it and find peace for your soul" (Jeremiah 6:16).*

> *"To the discerning man, the way of life leads upward; he will be saved from the underworld below" (Proverbs 15:24).*

14. Vision: A Sandbag Fell off the Truck While I Was Driving

October 11, 2017: date of the vision

On a Friday afternoon, I felt so tired after a day's work, and it got worse at the thought of the heavy traffic I anticipated facing at the peak hours of the day. It regularly takes me fifty minutes to reach home, but with traffic congestion, it can take up to one hour and twenty minutes. Apart from the long distance, this highway is considered one of the notorious motorways, based on numerous accidents recorded daily. Most of the motor vehicles seen on this highway are long-haul trucks, tautliners, commercial vans, and utility trucks. This had been my struggle for eleven years, since our company's distribution warehouse moved to the south-eastern part of the city in 2006. I hadn't started my day's work yet, and I already felt exhausted and stressed due to the anxiety over driving along this infamous motorway.

Because of the driving distance, it had been my daily routine to pray the Rosary on my way to work and back. As a driver for twenty-eight years now, I was blessed to be clear of any offenses. I believe that prayers settle down my nerves and keep me still and serene, so I ignored the bad drivers I encountered along the road and rather concentrated on my safe driving.

It was around five o'clock in the afternoon, and I was in the middle lane of the three-lane road. A small pick-up truck, or what's known as a "ute," was right in front of me. It was loaded with stacked sand bags, but I instantly noticed that they weren't securely tied in! *I envisioned one bag of sand falling off the truck!* Instinctively, I quickly moved to my left lane to avoid it. Not long after I had changed lanes, I heard a big bang sound and looked at my side mirror. I saw a domino-effect accident in the middle lane caused by *sand bags that had fallen off the truck, and not only one sandbag as I saw in my vision, but several of them!* The traffic flow started to build up quickly, and soon the blaring sounds of sirens were heard on both directions.

Interpretation and Realisation

This encounter was a straightforward and clear vision, which also happened right away. This kind of gift is called intuitive vision, which relates to intuition that is a spiritual gift. It's a feeling that something is true without conscious reasoning;

it's unexplainable, yet one feels or understands something instinctively without any proof or evidence. It's just a gut feeling. This pertains to one's presence and alertness of mind and deep concentration and focus on feelings and consciousness of one's surroundings. It's possible that all of us have the gift of intuition but only few are able to tap into it due to negligence or some kind of happy-go-lucky attitude.

When I envisioned that sandbag falling off, I acted quickly because I had that instinctive feeling that it would happen … and it did! I arrived home safe and sound. Praise God Almighty for your constant love and protection, as well as the angels and saints for shielding me from harm! Amen!

> *If you dwell in the shelter of the Most High and rest in the shadow of the Almighty, you can say to the Lord, "My stronghold, my refuge, my God in whom I trust!" (Psalm 91:1–2).*

15. Dream: Three Men with Black Hair Smiling at Me from a Distance

November 9, 2017: date of the dream

Last night I had a dream of three men with black hair smiling at me from a distance. I woke up feeling tired and completely puzzled. I said my usual morning prayers, ate breakfast, and drove to work. I offered the day praying to the Holy Spirit to give me some signs of the meaning of last night's dream.

As I was driving to work, I passed by one funeral car and immediately prayed for the soul of the dead. After twenty minutes, I passed by another hearse and prayed for the soul of the dead. Then just after the last traffic light before my workplace, I saw another funeral car! Again I prayed for the soul of the dead. I passed by three funeral cars in total!

Interpretation and Realisation

Here come some clues, like the connection of the three men and the three funeral cars on the road. At work, there was a hardworking old driver named Pietro, whom I also associated with my father in build and looks. At age sixty-eight, he still worked hard and didn't intend to retire. I asked him about it one time, and he told me that he'd keep working until he was flat dead on the ground! I'd noticed that like my father, he was a chain smoker, and occasionally I heard him coughing, which to me wasn't a good sign. Pietro was always included in my daily mass and prayers.

In our community, Stephen and I had connected with Philip, a very sickly man in his late sixties. He was one of the guitarists in the church choir. Every Sunday, we faithfully sang in the mass and felt the joy of service. Then we noticed his absence for almost two weeks. We checked on him and found out that he was hospitalized due to his underlying heart condition. His name was listed in my daily mass and prayers.

Sammy was sixty-four years old, the brother-in-law of our friend. He was diagnosed with prostate cancer a year ago and is now in palliative care at his own home. We were asked to say prayers for him and offer masses for peace and comfort. His name was also listed in my daily mass and prayers.

December 1: At work, our office manager broke the sad news that Pietro had passed away in the hospital. He had been suffering from lung cancer but totally ignored it. I later learned that he had to work hard to finish paying off their house to free his disabled wife from mortgage issues once he was gone. What a loving and responsible husband! May God bless his soul. Some legal advisers told him not to worry about anything, because his own superannuation fund would pay off his mortgage. He was so happy and relieved to get this information. I knew and felt that he had a peaceful death. May his soul rest in peace. Amen.

December 2: We received the sad news that Philip had died in the hospital. A week before, we had visited him after mass. Stephen, being an acolyte, had brought him a consecrated host. He was extremely delighted to receive the holy communion. In the Catholic Church, sick people receive the consecrated host, or holy communion, in their homes through the minister of the altar, or acolyte, and through the Eucharistic minister. He was happy to see us and chat with us, especially about his wife and daughter, who was still single at forty-three. He expressed his concern about them when he crossed the bar. We comforted him with our words of assurance that God would surely look after them. I knew and felt that he had a very peaceful death. May his soul rest in peace. Amen.

December 14: Our friend broke the sad news that his brother-in-law, Sammy, had passed away at home. He had struggled accepting death because he had some unfulfilled missions. His wife and four children were gathered around him. They prayed the Rosary and pleaded for God's mercy. His wife assured him that she would continue his unfinished mission. I knew and felt that he also died peacefully. May his soul rest in peace. Amen.

The reality of the dream of three men unfolded with the description of the men I mentioned above. *The three men were all smiling at me in the dream* symbolises peace and gratitude of daily prayers and masses faithfully offered for them. Prayers and masses are so powerful, especially when we pray and offer masses for the sick, elderly, oppressed, and the souls in purgatory. *The three funeral cars I passed by* represents these three men who all died and were showered with lots of prayers and masses. It made me feel so blessed and honoured to be an instrument for the peaceful death of each of them.

I dreamed of three men with black hair represents age. These three men had their own anxieties and worries about leaving their family due to reasons like unaccomplished missions, unpaid mortgages, and some more insecurities. They were all middle-aged and not ready to go yet, but illness overtook age. Death comes anytime, regardless of age, gender, and race. That's why there's the saying, "Young or old, be ready, for death is like a thief in the night."

Smiling at me from a distance represents time. There was an interval of days between the three men's deaths. Prayers and masses were continuously offered to them, even beyond life here on earth. I knew these prayers made them happy and thankful for this simple but sincere act of love.

> *Let the word of God dwell in you in all its richness. Teach and admonish one another with words of wisdom. With thankful hearts, sing to God psalms, hymns and spontaneous praise. And whatever you do or say, do it in the name of Jesus the Lord, giving thanks to God the Father through Him. (Colossians 3:16–17)*

> *"Return, O my soul, to your rest, for the Lord has been good to you" (Psalm 116:7).*

16. Dream: The Black Madonna's Picture on the Wall, Next to My New Manager's Desk

June 14, 2019: date of the dream

On a wintry night in June, I saw in my dream the picture of Our Lady, the Black Madonna, on the wall next to my new manager's desk! During this period of my life, two significant episodes took place on the same day at work and home.

In the first hour at work, an announcement was made that our new manager wanted to meet the whole department at lunch time. He humbly introduced himself and straight away made a very good impression on most of us, especially me. Though he wasn't old enough to be my father, I felt like I saw him as a fatherly figure when I met him. I was impressed with his family background and educational qualifications, which made me feel confident that he would be a big asset to our company's promising, bright future.

As soon as I got home that afternoon, I received a call from Jasmine, my eldest daughter, which was unusual because I knew she would be busy at work. She just casually checked on me to see if I was doing well, and then she said that she would drop by very soon. I got curious, since it was still early for her to leave work. With my intuition, I could feel something was wrong. After half an hour, she arrived at our house, and immediately I invited her to stay for dinner. I felt her restlessness and noticed that she constantly checked her mobile phone, as if she were expecting a message or a call. Then, unexpectedly, Lily, my youngest daughter, arrived too! That's it! I asked what was going on. They looked at each other, and Jasmine said, "Dad fainted at work and was rushed in an ambulance to the nearest hospital. Matthew is there with him now and just informed us of the good news that he's in stable condition. Mum, we didn't want you to get worried." We all hugged each other with tears of joy and thanked and praised God's love and protection toward Stephen. Praise God, oh Lord Almighty!

Our only son, Matthew, had been contacted instead of me, as per Stephen's instruction, because he didn't want me to get worried, due to my hypertension issue. Matthew immediately had driven to the hospital to check on his dad. When his dad was stabilised, he called his two sisters and told them what had happened! With peaceful hearts, the three of us eagerly went to visit him.

Our plan for that October was to join the Graces of Eastern Europe Pilgrimage as our last leg of the pilgrimage series. Stephen had to undergo many tests before getting a "go signal" to travel overseas. So we surrendered everything to God and focused on Stephen's medical tests. After two months (June and July) of tests, Stephen was finally given the clearance to travel. We were over the moon, and we praised and thanked the Lord for all the good results. Praise God to the heavens and earth for your power and glory!

During the first week of August, I made an appointment to meet up with my new manager, hoping I wasn't too late to apply for a leave in October. As I entered the manager's office, I prayed that everything would go well. Without any hesitancy, my new manager signed my leave application but asked me one major question: "Did I hear it right, that you intend to retire when you turn sixty-six?" That would be in twenty months' time. I simply but anxiously nodded in affirmation. He then solicited a big favour from me, which made me feel so humbled. He asked me not to retire or resign yet, even when I turned sixty-six. As a new manager, he needed my knowledge of the company's ins and outs. He probably needed some of my input and ideas acquired from thirty-one years of experience with the company. With full trust in him, I nodded again and left his room with peaceful heart.

Interpretation and Realisation

October 2019 was the culmination of our series of pilgrimages! We felt so blessed to join the Graces of Eastern Europe Tour at the last minute! This pilgrimage led us to major religious sites like the Shrine of Santo Nino of Prague, Our Lady of Czestochowa in Poland, Our Lady of Medjugorje in Bosnia, and Lake Bled's Church of Assumption in Slovenia, to mention a few.

My dream of the Black Madonna was clearly revealed when we went to Poland. I was ecstatic when I saw Our Lady of Czestochowa exactly the same as the Black Virgin I saw in my dream! I had to pinch myself to wake up, but this was now for real!

How about the picture on the wall next to my manager's desk? What was its significance? I firmly believed that Our Blessed Lady's intercessions for all our prayers and hearts' desires as a couple regarding our plans for future retirement would be granted, and that Our Blessed Lady would guide and hover over my manager for the best decision geared toward our advantage. It was the symbol of affirmation that everything would be fine. These were the words I felt Our Blessed Lady conveyed to me: "God showers you with endless blessings, more than what you have asked for. My Son knows all that is in your heart and soul. Trust Him."

Indeed, amazingly true! God gave everything and much more beyond our expectation! Stephen and I had completely and contentedly accomplished our bucket list on the series of pilgrimages, which had been our travel goal before retirement! May God be praised forever!

> *"From now on the Advocate, the Holy Spirit whom the Father will send in my name, will teach you all things and remind you of all that I have told you. Peace I leave with you, my peace I give you. Not as the world gives peace do I give it to you. Do not be troubled; do not be afraid" (John 14:26–27).*

17. Dream: A Man in a Bright-Coloured Polo Shirt Entered the Room

March 12, 2020: date of the dream

Due to the COVID-19 pandemic spreading around the world, the Australian government issued a stay-at-home order and restricted movement in order to cut down on the spread of the virus. Most workers worked from home, and only essential workers were permitted to go out. A few of us were asked to work from home, which I gratefully welcomed, as I was tired of long hours driving. Most importantly, Stephen wasn't in the best of health, and his doctor hadn't issued him clearance to go back to work due to his cough and cold, so this was convenient for us, to stay home together.

That night, I dreamed that there was a gathering of about twenty people, all cheerfully chatting. Some kids were running around the hall playing hide and seek, and the ladies were preparing the table with lots of food and drinks while the men put up some buntings or decorations on the wall. Everybody applauded as a man in bright-coloured polo shirt entered the room. What a colourful scene!

Interpretation and Realisation

When I woke up that beautiful and bright morning, the colourful scenery I saw in my dream lingered in my mind. I had goosebumps and tears of joy because I felt and knew that some memorable episodes were coming up in our lives! I experienced a total contrast of emotions as I watched and listened to the news about this dreaded deadly coronavirus called COVID-19 spreading all over the world. When Stephen reported to his HR department that he hadn't been given clearance from his doctor, he agreed to a non-paid leave due to his lack of sick leave and annual leave.

The next day, our family doctor called and shared the disappointing news that hubby had chronic bronchitis due to some inflammation along his bronchial tubes, which was causing his constant cough, chest discomfort, and breathing issues. Hence, our family doctor sadly was unable to issue him clearance to work for two reasons. First, Stephen's job location was in the cold storage of dairy products, which might worsen his medical condition. Secondly, with the pandemic crisis, no one was allowed to enter the premises with chronic bronchitis. I felt that God clearly conveyed His message to Stephen.

That night right after our Rosary prayers, hubby told me the much-awaited-words from his mouth: "God is telling me that now is the right time to retire!" Indeed! Even our children told him that at seventy years old, he's long overdue for retirement.

Stephen has been a hardworking man who started pasturing carabaos in the field at eight years old! Being one of fifteen children in a farming family, he had no choice but to help his father in order to have food on their table. Now that he had reached seventy, it was about time to "re-tyre" or "change tyres," just like the car tyres when moving to a slower pace or speed. It's time to enjoy but still be active physically and, especially, spiritually. It's the time to fully give back to God our time, talent, and treasure. It must be a balanced life of faith in service to God, family, and community. And we'll have fun fishing, gardening, and traveling. Stephen retired in May. Surprisingly, that same month my manager gave me the great news that I could retire at the financial year end in June! Thank you, oh Lord God Almighty!

In November 2020, gathering restrictions were lifted just in time for Stephen's birthday celebrations and the thanksgiving for our retirement! *This was exactly the joyful and jovial scene that appeared in my dream, and the man in bright and colourful polo shirt was none other than my husband!* Our whole family celebrated his seventieth birthday to the fullest, thanking and praising God for His unconditional love and faithfulness to all of us!

We praise and thank you, Lord, for your endless blessings and graces to us and our family!

> *"Rejoice always, pray without ceasing and give thanks to God at every moment. This is the will of God for you in Christ Jesus" (1 Thessalonians 5:16–18).*

18. Dream: My Cousin and I Dressed in White Gowns

April 19, 2020: date of the dream

One early cool autumn morning, I woke up to the sound of a siren from the motorway. I quickly sat on the bed and said my morning prayers. Then I happily recalled *my beautiful dream of my cousin, Lydia, and I, both dressed in white gowns. Such a solemn and sacred setting inside a high-ceilinged hall with antique chandeliers! Inside were many other ladies in white gowns and men in white polo shirts and black pants. Then a middle-aged lady, also dressed in white and holding some folders, called our names one by one and signalled us to stand at the front, facing the crowd.*

As I prepared our breakfast, I prayed and contemplated the meaning and significance of that beautiful dream.

Interpretation and Realisation

Lydia, who is a year older than me, is my first cousin. Her father was my mother's elder brother, who also died in his mid-fifties due to lung and heart issues. Due to her father's early death, and being the eldest daughter in the family, she became the family's bread winner. For greener pastures, she also migrated to Australia in 1988, just a few months ahead of us. She became engrossed with her work to keep up with the unending support for her brother and five sisters in the Philippines, and especially her sickly mother. Because of this sole responsibility on her shoulders, she completely ignored her love life and remained single the rest of her life. She unselfishly dedicated her whole life to her family's needs.

As first cousins, Lydia and I have a very close and loving relationship, even exceeding that of real sisters. In June 2011, my cousin called and asked if she could live with us. Without any hesitancy, especially since Stephen and I lived in an empty nest, we accepted her with open arms. From then on, the three of us had dinner together and told our stories and happenings of the day. Because we all worked full-time, dinner was our quality time for important updates and chats over a cup of tea. Then we'd pray the Rosary before retiring to bed. The topic of retirement came up in our conversations, and we both planned to be a catechist to introduce Jesus to the young children and deepen their faith and love for God.

After five-and-a-half years, Lydia heard the sad news about her sickly mother. She fervently prayed for discernment over whether to go home to the Philippines and look after her mother or continue working in Australia until retirement, which wasn't too far away. A firm decision was quickly made after being given all the signs from the Holy Spirit, as she confided to me.

In April 2017, she flew back home for good and joyfully looked after her mother. She said, "Life is too short; I'll make the most of it to be with her." For that decision, I honoured and saluted her. That's right! Money isn't all that matters; it's the love that you sincerely share and give. Saint Therese of the Child Jesus said, "Nothing is small in the eyes of God. Do all that you do with Love."

The following month, I received an email from Lydia saying that she had finished her training as a catechist and had started teaching in the elementary public school. She had successfully achieved her plan through God's graces and blessings!

By June 2020, Stephen and I had retired. Unfortunately, we couldn't go anywhere due to the pandemic around the world. We were in lockdown, and the Australian government issued stay-at-home orders. How could I attend training sessions on my mission of being a catechist in the middle of this lockdown? Thank goodness for the modern technology of Skype and Zoom meetings. I finished my training in Special Religious Education in two months! I am now a qualified catechist! Thank you, oh Lord!

The dream of my cousin and myself dressed in white gowns symbolises our purity of service and sincere devotion to give and share the gift of faith with the children, to help them know the one true God, Jesus Christ. We were in that *high-ceilinged hall with antique chandeliers*, which represented the height, or pinnacle, of this noble service and being witnesses to the gospel and ministers of the light of truth. Indeed, it is an honour to be called in this ministry! Thank you, Lord God, for calling us by name!

> *"If you have received Christ Jesus as Lord, continue to live in Him. Be rooted and built up in Him, strengthened in the faith as you were taught, overflowing with thankfulness" (Colossians 2:6–7).*

19. Dream: Tatay and His Usual Early Morning Coffee, Cigar, and Music

May 20, 2020: date of the dream

Thirty-three years ago this May, Tatay died of lung cancer at the age of sixty-one. One night we prayed the Rosary and offered mass for his death anniversary. After our daily 7:00 p.m. Rosary and night prayers before bed, I joyfully recollected Tatay's earthly life, and he appeared to me in my dream!

Tatay was so happy and smiling at every passer-by as he was seated near the wide capiz windows of our Spanish-style house with his usual early morning coffee and cigar while listening to his favourite music. I saw the shiny wooden floors of our big house, which Tatay loved brushing with coconut husks after applying floor wax. He was so joyful and energetic on an early morn.

This had been his routine every time he went home to our province on weekends, because he stayed in the city during the week and worked as a truck-broker at Manila Port. I woke up with tears of joy and thanksgiving for that beautiful setting! That place means a lot to me! Kuya Nico, Liam, and I were all born there, a lonely place where I grew up with a mixture of emotions and tons of trials, frustrations, and challenges. At the same time, it was a lovely place where I felt the hands of God and His unconditional love holding me and guiding me as His wings protected me from harm and vanity. I felt nostalgic and emotional as I seemed to smell the presence of God!

Interpretation and Realisation

Tatay went through the emotional trauma of losing his beloved wife of only ten years. It was an early and shocking death, and I felt so sad for Tatay, as he didn't accept the loss and move on with his life. He became a worrier, an alcoholic, and a chain smoker, which led to his dreadful lung cancer. But last night's dream had elated my spirit, for I visualised Tatay and Nanay together with my two brothers, Kuya Nico and Liam, in God's heavenly kingdom with the angels and saints. They were all joyful as one family in Heaven and, at the same time, extremely happy for us here on earth for our achievements in the midst of so many hardships and tribulations.

Coffee, cigars, and music are great partners that symbolise inner strength and power, a relaxed mind and spirit, and full satisfaction and purest contentment. I envisioned Tatay and Nanay smiling at me and saying, "Well done, our dearest and loving daughter, for taking care of your brothers. We love you so dearly." I closed my eyes and heard the voices of my two brothers gladly saying, "Thank you for your kindness and goodness of heart. You are the best sister in the whole wide world. We give you all our love and prayers." Tears of joy and peace continuously flowed down my cheeks as I exalted and magnified God's goodness!

> *"The Lord is my strength and my shield; in Him my heart trusts. I have been helped and my heart exalts, with my song I give Him thanks" (Psalm 28:7).*

20. Dream: An Old Man Served Us Bread, Butter, and Olives on a Big, Round Plate

December 1, 2020: date of the dream

As a couple, we were celebrating our half-year anniversary of being retirees and pensioners! What a great blessing and grace from God! Thank you, Lord God Almighty, for your generosity! The first day of December dawned bright and sunny, hubby and I attended the earliest mass as our thanksgiving for reaching that anniversary. After mass, we had breakfast at a nearby café and recollected all of God's faithfulness and generosity to us as a migrant family after thirty-two blessed years.

At the start of our retirement, we thought we'd be on a tight budget, but we were totally wrong! Our pantry has never been fuller! God has given us everything abundantly. Words are not enough to express our sincerest gratitude for all His goodness and divine providence for the whole family, our children, and grandchildren.

These ecstatic and highly emotional feelings that day continued through the night as I dreamed about this most unforgettable, amazing, and exceptional encounter. To this day, it's the most detailed and remarkable of all the dreams I've ever had!

The setting was back home in our native land of the Philippines, and our children were still very young at ages four, six, and eight. It was a bright sunny morning at the park, and the children were enjoying the different rides at the playground, like swings, slides, and mazes for kids. When they reached the fullest satisfaction in trying all the rides, each of them asked for food and drinks! So we walked toward the market and decided to have lunch in one of the local eateries nearby, as the children were tired of walking and we were all hungry. We saw a nipa-hut-sheltered table with long wooden benches on both sides. It was spacious enough for all of us. There were many other empty tables, but this one looked so inviting!

Then an old man came out of the kitchen with cold water and joyfully served us a big loaf of bread, butter, and olives and some delicious looking hot sausages on a big, round plate. There was more buttered slices of bread on the side! It looked great and delicious! The sausages were the kids' favourite, and the oven-scented freshly baked bread was really tempting, but hubby and I looked at each other puzzled, because we hadn't ordered yet. I was about to ask the old man about it, but he seemed to be in a rush. As he quickly turned around, I noticed that his hands were clasped together, and I saw some drops of blood. I thought that maybe he had an accidental cut on his hands, which was why he rushed to go until I couldn't see him anymore.

The children were so hungry and started eating while I pondered over this episode and, particularly, the drops of blood on the old man's hands. Then a middle-aged woman, who looked like she was the owner of the place, came out from the kitchen with a baffled look in her eyes and shockingly asked us, "Who served you?"

Interpretation and Realisation

I was confused and bewildered when I woke up, coupled with this indescribable feeling! After my morning prayers, I went to the garden for reflection as I recalled the details of the dream: *the old man serving us food, specifically bread, butter, olives, and sausages, which we did not order; he knew the kids' favourite food; the big, round plate; the drops of blood from his hands; his sudden disappearance; and the confused lady-owner!*

Then I closed my eyes and prayed for the Holy Spirit to come. Suddenly I felt ecstatic! With my heart throbbing fast, I felt the presence of God, smelled the burning incense in the air, and sensed the prompts from the Holy Spirit! "*Oh, my Lord Jesus was in my dream*!" *He* was the *old man* who served us the bread, butter, and olives! Oh Lord and my God!

Bread symbolises the sustenance of life, which gives spiritual enhancement. The more bread you eat, the more rich you'll become spiritually. *Bread* means the Word of God as our guide in life's journey. *Butter* represents a solid and steady mind fixed on God. *Olives* symbolise wisdom and peace, prosperity and success. *The big, round plate* symbolises harmony, protection, unity, commitment, and love. The *drops of blood from His hands* represent His unconditional love to all of us as our Saviour and Redeemer who died on the cross to save us from the damnation of sins! God is all-knowing. He knows our heart's desires and gives them to us in His own time and ways.

Tears of overwhelming joy fell down my cheeks; on my knees, I praised and thanked God for everything! In awe and ecstasy, I raised my hands to the heavens until I heard His voice: "I am always with you, all the way forever, and I will look after you till the end of the earth!"

> *"Have no fear, for I am with you; be not dismayed, for I am your God. I will give you strength, and bring you help, I will uphold you with my right hand of justice" (Isaiah 41:10).*

21. Dream: My Husband Slipped on the Altar in the Church Sanctuary and Fell on the Floor; Parishioners Rushed to Help Him

October 30, 2021: date of the dream

Early in June of 2021, an unvaccinated limousine driver from New South Wales tested positive for Covid and infected other residents, which resulted in a "fast and furious" spread of this fatal virus in the different places he'd visited. NSW got into the second wave of the pandemic, caused by the Delta variant, which was more contagious and fatal than the last year's strain of Covid-19.

The NSW Premier soon declared a lockdown in the affected Local Government Areas (LGA). Our suburb was also named as a "hotspot" area, so a mandated stay-home-order was issued. In order to minimise the movement of people, no one could go out except for essential food, medicine, medical check-ups, Covid tests, and vaccination. This mandate lasted for four months.

The hustling-bustling Greater Sydney Area turned into a ghost town, which was aggravated by a curfew in some areas from 9:00 p.m. to 5:00 a.m. Covid cases and deaths were reported daily, and people religiously tuned in every day at 11:00 a.m. for the update, with feelings of fear and hope. Many things were impacted, like job security, shop openings, people's mental and physical health, and relationship make or break situations.

During this depressing lockdown, I noticed Stephen's negativity in spite of our daily attendance at live stream masses. I started to analyse his actions and came to the conclusion that anxiety and depression were looming over him.

In this lockdown, we established a daily routine: 8:30 a.m. live stream mass, 10:30 a.m. brunch, household chores, our own home recreation, 5:00 p.m. early dinner, and ending the whole day with a 7:00 p.m. Rosary. Stephen's recreation was to sit and turn on the TV while also on his mobile's YouTube. He saw all the negativity of social media here in Australia and around the world. News of death, horrible crimes, domestic violence, murder, corruption, and other types of depressing news will make a normal person, abnormal!

Stephen is a fishing fanatic and was dying to go out and fish, but he didn't want to take the risk of paying $1,000 for the offense. I encouraged him to watch fishing expeditions around the world instead of the depressing news, and thankfully he did. I made time to watch with him so that I could understand his fishing passion. We also watched movies together, like inspirational success stories, comedies, and musicals, so we both shared this joy and laughter even in the midst of lockdown! I diligently kept an eye on him and fervently prayed for God's grace and touch of healing of his whole being.

Then finally, as of 12:01 a.m. on October 11, 2021, the NSW lockdown was officially lifted! This marked the end of 107 days of Covid lockdown. Thanks to the massive vaccination campaign of the government, and the cooperation of the people, which saw more than 70 per cent aged sixteen and over vaccinated, these restrictions ended. This became NSW's version of "Freedom-Day," which meant residents could socialise, dine out, and go shopping again but with Covid protocols still in place, like wearing a mask indoors, social distancing, and showing proof of double vaccination.

Freedom Day made way to finally opening churches and different places of worship again! Our own parish priest announced that on the last weekend of October, there would be masses, but people would still wear a mask and follow all the Covid protocols. Stephen and I were both over the moon when we heard the great news; we were so happy to be in church and serve again! We had been regular volunteers, opening the church for Sunday's earliest mass, and Stephen served as acolyte while

I served as a reader. Finally, we would be able to celebrate and receive the Holy Eucharist after 107 days of anxiety, boredom, and, most of all, fear of getting the virus!

That Saturday night after our 7:00 p.m. Rosary prayers, I went to bed, ready for the 5:30 a.m. alarm. On Sunday mornings, it had been our routine to leave at 6:30 a.m. to open the church and do all the necessary preparations for the 7:30 a.m. mass.

In the middle of the night, I woke up terrified and scared about what I'd dreamed! *My husband slipped on the church altar in the sanctuary and fell on the floor! I, together with the parishioners, rushed to help him.* That was a very concerning and alarming dream! What would it mean? Oh Most Holy Spirit, guide and enlighten me with your wisdom!

Interpretation and Realisation

Freedom Day! Finally, after 107 days, each NSW citizen rejoiced when the Premier announced the start of Freedom Day at 12:01 a.m. on October 11, 2021! Every Christian deprived of entering churches and places of worship would admit to the hunger and thirst each felt to personally attend masses and receive the Holy Eucharist! What a huge relief!

Stephen and I were both so excited to enter the church and serve in the mass, but my dream made me so anxious. On our way to church, I prayed to the Holy Spirit to guide and lead me, because I was so worried about Stephen. I knew he was so eager to serve again, but he still wasn't in the best of health. *During the mass, I observed every detail of what he was doing at the altar in order to warn him and avoid that alarming vision in my dream. To add to this feeling of anxiety, the other acolyte didn't turn up to help Stephen, so I doubled up my effort to assist him. I believed that Stephen wasn't alone around the altar serving but that the angels were joyfully assisting him! The mass started solemnly, and then I noticed the absence of the bell. It was just fifteen minutes before the Sanctus part of the mass, so I signalled Stephen to get the missing bell! The ringing of the bell is a crucial part of Sanctus! Whew! he just made it in the nick of time!*

The Sanctus ("Holy, Holy, Holy") is the most important of all the people's acclamations at the mass. It's meant to be a cheer, a joyful shout of thanks and praise to God! The ringing of the bell adds to the elated and ecstatic ambiance of the adoration to honour God's power and glory. The mass solemnly ended and everything went well. Stephen was saved from any harm and danger!

Slipped on the altar's sanctuary symbolises his non-observance of the missing bell. I was so thankful that my dream had truly alarmed me to be watchful of Stephen. Had I not noticed the absence of the bell, we would have missed the ambiance of the cheers and joy of the Sanctus, aside from his guilt over the failure to perform his utmost duty, especially as this was the first Sunday of freedom from lockdown.

The opening of churches and places of worship certainly devastated the side of darkness. God is always triumphant and victorious! *Parishioners rushing to help him* symbolised the angels' assistance around the table, as I firmly believed! Everything went perfectly well and not a single soul, including Stephen and the priest, noticed all that commotion and anxiety except God, the angels, and myself!

God clearly conveyed His message to me through that dream. I have to remain vigilant, cautious, and supportive of my husband, for He chose us to be His faithful disciples and followers!

Thank you and praise to you, King of Kings, Lord of Lords, oh Lord God Almighty!

> *"LORD, you are my God; I will exalt you and praise Your Name, for You have done wonderful things, things planned long time ago, faithful and true" (Isaiah 25:1).*

This is the end of this journey for now! Hope you've enjoyed the ride! As long as we breathe and live, we keep dreaming and having visions. So with God's graces and blessings, until we meet again in the next episodes!

Lanni Fides

Conclusion

It's my sincerest hope that you have learned something from this book, especially the main point of listening to God's messages through dreams and visions. These can change and empower your lives, as proven in all the encounters I have cited, together with my own experiences. You have seen the importance of acknowledging dreams and visions and constantly seeking the guidance of the Holy Spirit for the gift of understanding and interpretation of these encounters with God.

Aside from believing and accepting this, we must exert our best efforts to stay connected with God. With the busyness of the world due to earthly ambitions like fame, wealth, and power, we tend to forget God and thus fall into the trap of destruction. Nowadays, seated comfortably at home, distance is no longer a hindrance from attending world conventions, conferences, and meetings, as well as training sessions and home learning, because of the modern technology of Skype, Messenger chats, Zoom, Google Meet, etc.

This is the danger zone, because this is the point where we lose our connection with *Him*! We are deaf when He calls; we can't hear His voice when He speaks to us due to the noise of hustle and bustle of earthly demands. We're blind when He is in front of us; we can't see Him due to endless distractions. This is the spot where we lose the plot. We now view dreams and visions as irrelevant in our lives!

Remain securely strapped to and strongly linked with God; we can't be loosely connected or halfway-connected, but we must be fully and totally connected 24/7. How can we do this? All is possible when there's a will. Keep the link with God firm and strong through daily prayers, attendance at holy retreats, participation in groups with the same faith, and involvement in community and church services. These avenues lead us to the right course and stop us from destruction and derailment.

First and foremost, always P R A Y unceasingly.

P—Praise God with all our minds, with all our hearts, and with all our souls.

R—Repent and acknowledge that we are sinners; we ask for God's mercy and forgiveness for our sins and wrongdoings.

A—Ask and seek the power of the Holy Spirit to dwell upon us always in order to be guided in the right direction.

Y—Yield to God's will and ways, not our ways, as shown in the passage below.

"Trust in the Lord with all your heart; do not rely on your own insight. Let His presence pervade all your ways, and He will make your paths smooth" (Proverbs 3:5–6).

Through prayer, we are closely linked with God, for we are lifted up to the heavens!

Lastly, dear readers, with deep humility I extend my utmost gratitude for spending time reading this book. I sincerely hope that you have enjoyed and gained satisfaction from it, and most of all discovered your spiritual gifts; if not, aim and pray to be able to know them. Use the spiritual gifts you have discovered to glorify God's faithfulness and goodness. Be keen to listen to God's messages when He speaks to you through dreams and conveys instructions through visions. In doing so, you are going in the right direction of your life's journey!

I'll leave you with one last quotation, which I learned from a German nun from the Order of Saint Benedict in 1975: "A beautiful life does not just happen. It is built daily by prayers, humility, sacrifices and love."

Rest assured that you are always in my prayers, and I humbly request that you pray for me too. May God's graces and blessing be with you forever and ever! Amen! Amen! Amen!

Lanni Fides
December 22, 2021

Endnotes

https://www.africa.thegospelcoalition.org/dream-vision
- (2 June 2021) – Ch.1.2

https://www.amazingbibletimeline.com/blog/jacob
- (28 June 2021) – Ch.3.1a

https://www.amazingbibletimeline.com/blog/joseph-in-egypt
- (2 Aug 2021) – Ch.3.1b

https://www.beliefnet.com.faiths/christianity/what-the-bible -really-says-about-dreams-and-visions
- (2 June 2021) – Ch.1.2

https://www.beliefnet.com/faiths/christianity
- (12, 13 June 2021) – Ch.2.1-3

https://www.bible.org/illustration/eleven-visions-god
- (9 Sept 2021) – Ch.3.2a-e

http://www.bornofwonder.com/home/the-dreams-of-st-joseph
- (2 Aug 2021) – Ch.3.1b

https://www.britannica.com/biography/joseph-biblical-figure
- (2 Aug 2021) – Ch.3.1b

https://www.britannica.com/biography/moses-hebrew-prophet
- (12 Sept 2021) – Ch.3.2a

https://www.catholicexchange.com/the-early-visions-of-st-teres
a-of-kolkata
- (29 Aug 2021) – Ch.3.1e

https://www.catholicnewsagency.com/saint/st-teresa-of
-kolkata-585
- (29 Aug 2021) – Ch.3.1e

https://www.catholic.org/saints/saint.php?saint_id=5611
- (30 Aug 2021) – Ch.3.1e

https://www.christianitytoday.com/history/people/movers
andshakers/francis-of-assisi.html
- (23 Aug 2021) – Ch.3.1d

https://www.dictionary.cambridge.org/vision
- (1 June 2021) – Ch.1.2

https://www.differencebetween.info/difference-between
-vision-and-dream
- (1 June 2021) – Ch.1.2

https://www.en.m.wikipedia.org/wiki/Mother_Teresa
- (29 Aug 2021) – Ch.3.1e

https://www.en.m.wikipedia.org/wiki/Moses
- (12 Sept 2021) – Ch.3.2a

https://www.en.m.wikipedia.org/wiki/Isaiah
- (14 Sept 2021) – Ch.3.2b

https://www.e.m.wikipidia.org/wiki/Ezekiel
- (16 Sept 2021) – Ch.3.2c

https://www.en.m.wikipedia.org/wiki/Saint_Stephen
- (17 Sept 2021) – Ch.3.2d

https://www.en.m.wikipedia.org/wiki/John_the_Apostle
- (21 sept 2021) – Ch.3.2e

https://www.franciscanmedia.org/saint-of-the-day/saint-francis-of-assisi
- (23 Aug 2021) – Ch.3.1d

https://www.franciscanmedia.org/franciscan-spirit-blog/st-francis-and-his-dreams
- (23 Aug 2021) – Ch.3.1d

https://www.mintools.com/gifts-list

- (2 June 2021) – Ch.2.1

http://www.neverthirsty.org/bible/question/what-is-jacobs-ladder-all-about

- (28 June 2021) – Ch.3.1a

ABOUT THE AUTHOR

Lanni Fides is a former high school teacher-librarian and college professor who migrated from the Philippines to Australia with her family in 1988. In 1991, the family joined Couples for Christ, NSW Australia, became a couple-leader of a mission team to the northern region of Couples for Christ, and a coordinator of NSW Handmaids of the Lord, a ministry for women of the community. Currently, she is still an active member of the seniors' group in her community.

As a retiree, she's an active servant of St. John 23rd Parish, Stanhope Gardens, NSW, and a catechist of the state schools of the parish under the Ministry of Special Religious Education of the Diocese.

Her main mission in writing books is to proclaim God's unconditional love and faithfulness to His people.

"Have no fear, for I am with you; be not dismayed, for I am your God. I will give you strength, and bring you help, I will uphold you with my right hand of justice" (Isaiah 41:10).

God never leaves us; it is us who leave Him.

Lanni Fides
22.12.21

CPSIA information can be obtained
at www.ICGtesting.com
Printed in the USA
LVHW100739260422
717138LV00006B/239

9 780228 873211